THE SECOND OSWALD

Could Lee Harvey Oswald have fired 3 shots in 5.6 seconds with the inaccurate rifle he had—and hit a moving target? Did he even kill patrolman Tippit (the bullets in the body were smaller than the barrel of his revolver)? Was the brown paper bag made only to attract attention? Was Bullet No. 399 a plant? Suppose there was a *Second Oswald*—a man very similar physically and an expert marksman? Such a man was seen both before and at the time of the murder. Was there a rifleman on the knoll as well as at the Book Depository window?

If so, this is one of the greatest—and most successful conspiracies of modern times ...

The Second Oswald has been called "the first plausible and significant argumentation on the Kennedy assassination". It takes into account the recent books by Edward J. Epstein, Mark Lane and Harold Weisberg. Its author, Professor Richard H. Popkin, was Chairman of the Department of Philosophy at the University of California. He goes beyond criticism of the Warren Report, to propound a theory of what actually happened on that fatal 22nd November in 1963.

The Second Oswald becomes timelier with each passing year. The shortcomings of the Warren Commission report have been well established, but too often, sensationalistic and even absurd counter-theories have been offered. Unlike so many other books regarding the assassination, *The Second Oswald* is careful to discount the official story--and equally careful not to offer conclusions that cannot be supported by credible evidence.

The Second Oswald

Richard H. Popkin

Introduction by Murray Kempton

An imprint of C & M Online Media
Raleigh, North Carolina

Published by **Boson Books**
Raleigh, North Carolina

ISBN 1-932482-33-4
An imprint of **C&M Online Media, Inc.**
Copyright 1996, 2006 Richard H. Popkin
Cover art by Joel Barr
www.joelbarr.com

Design by Once Removed

www.bosonbooks.com

Acknowledgements

I should like to take this opportunity to thank various people who have helped me in the preparation of this book. First, Mr. Robert Silvers of the New York Review of Books for his editorial assistance. I wish also to thank Professor Stuart Hampshire for suggesting that I write the book, and Professor Daniel Gillis, Mr. Paul Hoch, Mr. Jones Harris, Mrs. Sylvia Meagher, and Professor Leonora Cohen Rosenfield for their kindness in supplying me with information after the case, especially while I have been abroad. I want also to thank the many people who have written to me with suggestions. Unfortunately I have not been able to write to them all personally, and so I take this opportunity to express my appreciation for their interest and ideas. I should also like to thank my colleagues in La Jolla for their patience in listening to me for many, many months on the subject, and for their helpful suggestions and criticisms. And I wish to thank the British Museum for the use of their set of the 26 volumes of the Warren Commission findings which they put at my disposition while I was working in London. And thanks to my family for their assistance, their patience and their fortitude, especially my wife, Juliet, for her editorial help, and my daughter Margaret for catching an egregious error in the galleys.

Richard H. Popkin
Paris
October 31, 1966

CONTENTS

Introduction

Dr. Popkin's small book brings us to the third stage of a great case that is never, one fears, to be formally tried but which endures enough to be endlessly cast over in the public mind. So it deserves annotation as though it were a real case, indeed as The Matter of the United States vs. The Ghost of Lee Harvey Oswald.

For the adversary system of justice is a very tough old dog, even when suspended by the Chief Justice of the United States. The question of whether a dead man deserves a defense in court seems at first thought a trivial one to the utilitarian mind, since the best advocate can give such a defendant no very tangible service. And yet the whole history of U.S. vs. Ghost of Oswald makes a strong argument that the adversary system has one special utility: there is no other way to arrive at any finding which can long persuade us that it is the truth.

1) The first stage of the case was assumed by the court to be the last; it was the issuance over Chief Justice Warren's signature of The Report of the President's Commission on the Assassination of President Kennedy.

That was, in essence, the case against Oswald's memory as gathered by the police and prepared for trial by the prosecution. It was as persuasive as statements for the prosecution usually are when the trial begins; and it carried singular weight because there would never be a trial. There has ever since been the assumption that the Warren Commission Report was universally accepted as a final judgment by all persons except the most alienated. This is not quite true; there were criticisms at the beginning. It was not ever possible to read these findings without becoming at once aware of the special defects of the prosecutor's mind. I myself was able, on the day the Report was issued, publicly to set down ten examples of the unfairness which is built into the business of making any case—a special kindness to the contradictions of one's own witnesses and a cold dismissal of any witness whose recollections might not fit the carpentry; a fondness for any colorful detail, however implausible, because colorful detail seems so circumstantial; the use of tests whose only purpose was to elevate the implausible into the probable and therefore had to be defective in their conception. I mention this less because I am proud of my acumen than because I remain puzzled that persons I generally assume to be my betters did not at once recognize anything so obvious as this was. I have since been confirmed in my low opinion of the critical faculties necessary to this judgment by reading over what I wrote at the time; my strictures, while sound enough, were by no means so deep or so substantive as those of persons who worked upon the text longer and with more absorption.

I did not question either the autopsy or the ballistics evidence, for example; I have so abiding, although unbased, a faith in such things that I did not look at the exhibits. And having understood that it was impossible that such things would be faked, I quite neglected to recognize anything so obvious as the fact that a mind as closed as the Warren Commission's clearly was might read them with disabling prejudice. For, after all, like most of us, I believed that Lee Oswald was guilty alone—partly because any alternative seemed impossible and partly because any alternative was so uncomfortable. My only concern was a fair trial for Oswald's ghost; and it was an especially comfortable concern because it was assured that a fair trial would find him guilty.

2) So there was never any substantial reason to congratulate the Warren Commission for its performance; after saying that,

however, the mind did not automatically move to the duty of trying the job itself. To say that the Report was not objective is, after all, no terribly compelling argument; the prosecution is not required to be objective. The second stage of the trial—the one that counts—is the discovery that the prosecution has not been honest. That stage was a long time appearing; we owe its achievement almost exclusively to the work of Edward Jay Epstein whose Inquest was published by Viking this year and who receives his thoroughly deserved appreciation from Dr. Popkin in these pages.

Epstein did what every troubled journalist should have done; he went beyond the deficiencies of the document to examine the deficiencies of the men responsible for its preparation. They were men with far fewer deficiencies than the rest of us; it is, for example, curious enough to be crucial to our understanding that the statement of the case against Oswald, loaded with only the flimsiest attempt at concealment, was written by Norman Redlich, of the New York University Law School, a man who, in other circumstances, has demonstrated the noblest passion for the rights of the defendant and who can be trusted, in any other case, to go on demonstrating it for the rest of his life.

If Redlich could suspend the standards of his life in the service of the national compulsion to dispose of this horror as the act of one deranged outsider, it is difficult to think of any lawyer who would not. Actually, Redlich and other members of the staff were handicapped by the very condition that so much of their previous experience had been with the defense; they did not know enough about the function of prosecutors to avoid even those rashnesses against which the better district attorneys have learned to protect themselves.

Epstein's report of the recollections of the Commission's staff is of men, driven to wind up their business, without time or inclination to examine alternatives to the theory they brought to the case, with no thought of anything except to make the pieces fit and to persuade, even when they knew nothing that gave them the right to do more than surmise. The result is more destructive of the

Commission's case than if it had never tried to seal the case at all. When witnesses are seen to have been believed for reasons of convenience rather than of notable credibility, an overwhelming curiosity arises about those witnesses who were not believed because their testimony happened to be so inconvenient. In truth, nearly every witness in this case has now become as good as any other; our only duty is to bring a standard for credibility to the dissenting witnesses higher than the Commission established for its corroborating ones. For, if the Commission had not, from its inner necessity, disregarded the incontestable fact that the witnesses Howard Brennan, Marina Oswald, and Helen Markham had each lied to an agent of the investigation at one time or another, it would have had almost no spoken case at all.

Some of the mute witnesses have been left in no better condition. When Dr. Popkin argues, for example, that the spent bullet, essential to support the Commission's argument, could not have traveled the path imputed to it and been left in the almost intact condition in which it was found, he has taken the theory that Oswald acted alone, difficult to believe at best, and rendered it close to impossible.

3) So now we arrive at the third stage of U.S. vs. Ghost, so unexpectedly continuing—the presentation of the defense's alternative theory of the crime. It is not, to be sure, a complete statement of the defense; neither Popkin nor Epstein believes that the event could have been accomplished without some complicity on Oswald's part.

Once persuaded that the Commission's standards for the witnesses it accepted were fatally defective, we have no alternative in conscience except to begin to hear out those witnesses it rejected. Among these discards, Popkin fixes upon approximately a dozen witnesses who remembered meeting Oswald under circumstances often highly suggestive of his guilt. The Commission decided to disbelieve them all, for one reason or another, generally because Oswald could not have been in the place where they had seen him. In any great case there are persons whom the vagrant air infects with the memory that they have seen the suspect, but a majority of these witnesses do not read like persons of that sort and the mystery of their hallucination survives its dismissal by the Commission.

Now Popkin wonders whether these stories are true and whether or not there was someone who looked very much like the real Oswald and who made it his business to call what, after the fact, would certainly be suspicious attention to him. From here Popkin makes the leap to the theory that the two Oswalds were together at the Texas Book Depository and that each played his part in the assassination.

It can be argued that this is a theory very much in the key of those constructed in the older mystery stories as the answer with which the amateur detective confounds the professional. But this happens to be a case where the professionals have forfeited their right to be contemptuous of the deductions of philosophers; by now, the various stages of the process have so discredited the Warren Commission as to leave its case much less plausible than Popkin's theory.

When the empiric evidence is finally seen as incapable of accounting for the circumstances, the speculative mind can only construct a new hypothesis and begin again with the empiric evidence. Dr. Popkin has begun that process, and his hypothesis already accounts for more of the unaccountable than the Commission's does.

It lacks, of course, the finality of the Commission's original judgment; it sets us instead to traveling towards terrible unknowns. No wish for finality, however intense, can substitute for its achievement. The trip will have to be made, and it will be the more difficult and untidy because the Warren Commission was so desperate to be neat. But the adversary tradition, even when neglected, has a way of insisting on its rights.

Murray Kempton

One

The Theory That Everyone Accepted

In one of Victor Serge's last works, *The Case of Comrade Tulayev*, written over fifteen years ago, the Russian equivalent of the Oswald story is set forth. An alienated young man unhappy with the many aspects of his life in the Soviet Union—the food, his room, his job, etc.—acquires a gun, and manages to shoot Commissar Tulayev one night when he is getting out of a car. An extensive investigation sets in, followed by an extensive purge. Millions of people are arrested and made to confess to being part of a vast conspiracy against the government. The actual assassin is, of course, never suspected, since no one can imagine him as a conspirator. He continues to lead his alienated unhappy life, while the government uncovers the great plot.

In contrast when John F. Kennedy was assassinated a solution emerged within hours; one lonely alienated man had done the deed all by himself. The investigation by the Dallas Police and the FBI then proceeded to buttress this view, and to accumulate all sorts of details about the lone assassin, some false (like the murder map), some trivial (like his early school records), some suggestive (like the bag he carried into the Book Depository), some convincing (like the presence of his rifle and the three shells). From its origins in Dallas on the night of

November 22, 1963, the career of the theory of a single conspirator indicates that this was the sort of explanation most congenial to the investigators and the public (although the strange investigation of Joe Molina, a clerk in the Book Depository, from 2 A.M. November 23 until the end of that day, mainly for his activities in a slightly left-wing veterans' organization, suggests a conspiratorial interpretation was then under consideration).

The Warren Commission, after many months of supposed labor and search, came out with an anticlimactic conclusion, practically the same as that reached by the FBI in its report of December 9, 1963, except for details as to how it happened. The Commission, clothed in the imposing dignity of its august members, declared its conviction that one lone alienated assassin, Lee Harvey Oswald, had indeed carried out the crime.

The ready acceptance of this by then expected finding by the press and the public—except for a few critics—suggests that the American public got the kind of explanation it wanted, and perhaps deserved. For almost everyone the points that suggested a conspiratorial explanation were either disposed of by the "careful" work of the Warren Commission and the FBI, or by a faith that had grown up about the Report. Some of the early critical questions suggesting a conspiratorial explanation (raised by Buchanan, Joesten, Bertrand Russell, Trevor-Roper, etc.) were shown to be based on misinformation or misunderstandings, the result mainly of what the Dallas Police and the District Attorney had said, or what had appeared in newspaper accounts and interviews.

Other questions, based on the Report itself and what it failed to resolve (raised by Leo Sauvage, Salandria, Sylvan Fox, Mark Lane, etc.), were swept aside by faith—faith, first of all, that these matters must have been settled by the mass of data in the twenty-six supplementary volumes of testimony, depositions, and documents. The twenty-six volumes seemed to be so imposing, and were, in fact, so impenetrable, that they resolved most doubts. Finally, as Dwight Macdonald pointed out, if the critics of the Report and of the evidence in the twenty-six volumes supposedly supporting it managed to reveal how tendentious, one-sided, and inadequate some of the solutions were, the ultimate faith of the public rested on the integrity of Justice Warren and his fellow commissioners, the capabilities of the FBI and of the Commission lawyers. It was just too implausible that such irreproachable talent could have doctored the case or have come to the wrong conclusion.

Serge's Russia could only see an assassination as part of a grand conspiracy. The western European critics can only see Kennedy's assassination as part of a subtle conspiracy, involving perhaps some of the Dallas Police, the FBI, the right-wing lunatic fringe in Dallas, or perhaps even (in rumors I have often heard) Kennedy's successor. Thomas Buchanan, in his otherwise far-fetched work, *Who Killed Kennedy?*, shows that it is part of the American tradition to regard Presidential assassination as the work of one lone nut, no matter how much evidence there may be to the contrary although of course, this does not mean that some of the assassination attempts were not the work of lone, mad people, doing the whole job by themselves.

There seems to have been an overwhelming national need to interpret Kennedy's demise in this way, and thus the irresistible premise of the investigators, almost from the outset, was that Oswald did it all, all by himself (as Ruby was believed to have done it all, all by himself). Congressman Ford's book, *Portrait of an Assassin*, is a valiant and not entirely unsuccessful effort to make the thesis psychologically plausible by constructing an Oswald in turmoil looking for his moment of glory. Representative Ford also goes so far as to blame the conspiracy theories on one lone woman, Mrs. Marguerite Oswald, and to act as if there were no reason whatever, save for the alienated confused mind of Mrs. Oswald, Senior, even to doubt that one lone assassin thesis.

However, the "official" theory was in many ways implausible. It involved a fantastic amount of luck. If the FBI and Warren Commission reconstructions were correct, Oswald had to get the rifle into the building without attracting attention. Only two people saw him with a long package, and none saw him with it or the rifle in the building. He had to find a place from which he could shoot unobserved. The place, according to the "official theory," was observed until just a few minutes before the shooting. He had to fire a cheap rifle with a

distorted sight and old ammunition, at a moving target in minimal
time, and shoot with extraordinary accuracy (three hits in three shots,
in 5.6 seconds, according to the FBI; two hits in three shots in 5.6
seconds, according to the Commission).

If the "official theory" of the Commission is right, Oswald had no
access to the rifle from mid-September until the night before the
assassination (since the rifle was transported by Mrs. Paine from New
Orleans to Dallas, and thereafter was in the Paines' garage) and had
no opportunity whatsoever to practise for at least two months. Having
achieved such amazing success with his three shots, Oswald then was
somehow able to leave the scene of the crime casually and unobserved,
go home, and escape. But for the inexplicable (according to the "official
theory") Tippit episode, Oswald might have been able to disappear. In
fact, he did so after that episode, and only attracted attention again
because he dashed into a movie theater without paying.

The critics have argued that the Commission's case against
Oswald, if it had ever been taken to court, would have collapsed for
lack of legal evidence. A legal case would have been weakened by
sloppy police work (e.g., the failure to check whether Oswald's gun had
been used that day), confused and contradictory reports by witnesses
(e.g., the mistaken identification of Oswald by the bus driver), and
questionable reconstructions by the Commission (e.g., testing the accuracy of the rifle with stationary targets).

Mark Lane, for example, in his uneven work, *Rush to Judgment*,
indicates many of the points a clever defense attorney might have
raised, some of which would probably have caused serious damage to
the prosecution case against Oswald. The Report (against the better
judgment of at least two of the Commission's staff, Liebeler and Ball)
had to rely on some of the shakiest witnesses, like Brennan and Mrs.
Markham. It also had to impeach some of its best, like Wesley Frazier.

The critics were still dismissed. This was not, I suspect, simply because it was more difficult to believe that the Commission, its staff,
and the FBI could be in error than it was to accept a counter-
explanation, as Dwight Macdonald contended in *Esquire*. It was also

because the critics had no counter-theory that was better than science fiction, no explanation less implausible than that of the Report.

Two books recently published move the discussion to a new level. Harold Weisberg's noisy, tendentious *Whitewash* (which, for some good and probably many bad editorial reasons, no publisher would touch) is nevertheless the first critical study based on a close analysis of the twenty-six volumes themselves. Edward Jay Epstein's *Inquest*, a remarkably effective book, presents startling new data about the internal workings of the Commission. In addition, two recent articles by Vincent Salandria in *The Minority of One* and those by Fred Cook in *The Nation* raise important questions. This material suggests not that the "official theory" is implausible, or improbable, or that it is not legally convincing, but that by reasonable standards accepted by thoughtful men, it is impossible, and that data collected by the FBI and the Commission show this to be the case.

Before these writings appeared, there were already strong reasons for doubting that Oswald did the shooting alone, or at all. The majority of eye- and ear-witnesses who had clear opinions as to the origins of the shots thought the first shot was from the knoll or the overpass (and these witnesses included such experienced hands as Sheriff Decker, the Sheriff's men standing on Houston Street, diagonally across from the Book Depository, Secret Service Agent Sorrels, and many others). All of the Commission's obfuscation notwithstanding, Oswald was a poor shot and his rifle was inaccurate. The Commission tried hard to account for Oswald's very poor score on his last shooting test in the Marines. They got their expert witness to say that it might have been due to the poor atmospheric conditions at the time. "It might well have been a bad day for firing the rifle—windy, rainy, dark." (XI:304) The much maligned Mark Lane took the trouble to check on this, and reports in *Rush to Judgment*, p. 124, that the weather on that day in the Los Angeles' area, where the test occurred, was sunny and bright, and that there was no rain.

Experts could not duplicate the alleged feat of two hits out of three shots in 5.6 seconds, even though they were given stationary targets and ample time to aim the first shot, and had partially corrected the inaccuracy of the sight for the test. Furthermore, no reliable witness could identify Oswald as the marksman. No one saw him at the alleged scene of the crime, except Brennan, who did not identify him later on in a line-up. Hardly enough time was available for Oswald to hide the rifle and descend to the second floor, where he was seen by Policeman Baker.

No one saw or heard Oswald descend. And a paraffin test taken later that day showed positive results for nitrate on Oswald's hands, but negative ones on his cheek. All of this indicates that Perry Mason, Melvin Belli, or maybe even Mark Lane himself could have caused jurors to have reasonable doubts that Oswald did the shooting, or did all of the shooting. But none of this shows absolutely that Oswald could not have done it. He might have had fantastic skill and miraculous luck that day, and might have outdone the experts. He had an amazing talent for getting from place to place unobserved and unaccountably, and it could have been successfully employed at this time. The FBI and the Commission tell us a paraffin test is inconclusive (but then why do police forces use it?).

The "hard" data relied on by the Commission are that Kennedy was hit twice and Connally at least once; that Oswald's rifle was found on the sixth floor; that three shells ejected from Oswald's rifle were found by the southeast window of the sixth floor; that Oswald's palm print is on an unexposed portion of the rifle; that his prints are on some of the boxes found near the window; that ballistics experts say that the distorted bullet fragments found in Kennedy's car are from Oswald's rifle; that the almost complete bullet No. 399 found in Parkland Hospital (whose strange history and role will be discussed later) was definitely shot from Oswald's rifle; that Oswald was observed by at least five people in the building between 12:00 and 12:30, plus or minus a few minutes—two saw him on the first floor around noon, two report him on the fifth and sixth floor around this time, and Baker saw him right after the assassination on the second floor; and that Oswald left the building around 12:33 and went to Oak Cliff. (One might add some of the data on Tippit's murder as "hard fact," but Oswald's role in this incident is too much in dispute.) All of this certainly made a suggestive case that, difficulties notwithstanding, all of the shooting—three shots—was done by Oswald with his own rifle.

The material presented by Epstein and Salandria, and to a lesser extent by Cook and Weisberg, undermines the Commission's case in two ways. First, they closely examine both the sequence of the shots and the available medical evidence in order to demonstrate that all three shots could not have been fired by Oswald. Secondly, they show that the Commission's theory is in conflict with the FBI's on a number of crucial points: Indeed, one can only conclude either that both theories, considered together, are impossible, or that they establish that more than one assassin was firing at the President.

Two

The FBI Reports and Zapruder's Film

Two of the most important pieces of evidence undermining the "official theory" are the FBI'S Summary reports on the case and the film taken by Abraham Zapruder, a bystander during the assassination. The FBI's first summary report was dated December 9, 1963, just after the Warren Commission was appointed. The report is not in the twenty-six volumes and is published for the first time, and only in part, in Epstein's book. In it, the FBI states simply that "three shots rang out. Two bullets struck Kennedy and one wounded Governor Connally." This seemed to account for all the wounds; but it ignored incontrovertible evidence that one shot missed the car and its occupants and wounded a spectator.

As Epstein shows, this fact, and the evidence of the Zapruder film, forced the Commission to reconsider the problem. For the film established the time when Kennedy could have been hit, and when Connally could have been hit. The speed of Zapruder's camera is 18.3 frames per second and his film shows that Kennedy was hit between frames 208 and 225. (For reasons never explained, the Commission omitted Frames 208-211 from its reproduction of the series in its exhibits.) It seems from the medical and photographic evidence that

Connally was shot between frames 231 and 240. Some people suggest
it was either earlier or later, but the most likely possibility appears to
be in this interval. (The shot that struck Kennedy on the side of the
head and killed him was at frame 313.) This leaves less than 2.3
seconds between shots one and two; and the Commission found that it
is physically impossible to pull the bolt and reload Oswald's rifle faster
than once every 2.3 seconds (without aiming). Therefore it was
impossible for Oswald to have wounded both the President and
Connally in separate shots.

Epstein writes that, in early March, Arlen Specter, a Commission
lawyer, discussed this time problem informally with Commanders
Humes and Boswell, the Navy doctors who had performed the autopsy
on President Kennedy. "According to Specter, Commander Humes
suggested that since both Kennedy and Connally apparently had been
hit within a second of each other, it was medically possible that both
men had been hit by the same bullet and that Connally had had a delayed reaction. This hypothesis would explain how both men were
wounded in less time than that in which the murder weapon could be
fired twice ..." (*Inquest*, p. 115).

On March 16, 1964, when Dr. Humes's undated autopsy report was
first introduced in evidence, it directly contradicted both the FBI report of December 9, 1963, and the subsequent FBI report of January
13, 1964. Dr. Humes's report stated that the first bullet struck the
back of Kennedy's neck and exited through his throat. "The missile
contused the strap muscle on the right side of the neck, damaged the
trachea and made its exit through the anterior surface of the neck"
(Report, p. 543). Commander Humes, in his testimony, referred to the
place of entrance of the bullet as the low neck (II: 351). The FBI had
said, "Medical examination of the President's body had revealed that
the bullet which entered his back penetrated to a distance of less than
a finger length" (Exhibits 59 and 60).

These exhibits, reproduced in Epstein's book on pp. 56-57, are photographs of Kennedy's jacket and shirt. They show clearly a bullet hole
5 3/8 to 5 3/4 inches below the neckline, i.e., in his back. If the bullet
had been shot from the Book Depository, it was on a downward course,

and thus could not enter the back and exit through the throat unless it was deflected. Further, the FBI report had said, "Medical examination of the President's body revealed that one of the bullets had entered just below his shoulder to the right of the spinal column at an angle of 45 to 60 degrees downward, that there was no point of exit, and that the bullet was not in the body."

If the FBI data are correct, then Kennedy and Connally were hit by separate bullets and the time interval between these shots is much too short (less than two seconds) for both to have been fired from Oswald's rifle. Hence, either another gun was employed, or two different marksmen were shooting. In either case, the Commission theory is no longer tenable, nor, in view of the time-interval problem, is the theory of the FBI that all the shots came from Oswald's rifle. In response to Epstein's book, Commission staff members have stated that the two FBI reports of December 9th and January 13th are wrong about the wounds, while spokesmen for the FBI have implied, in more ambiguous language, that their reports were in error. Even before publication, Epstein's book had the effect of bringing a lot of information to light. Besides the portions of the FBI reports he has published, newspaper and magazine accounts have given the FBI explanations and the history of the autopsy report, etc., items which the Commission did not bother to clarify. If the FBI did make a mistake, one explanation may be found in Fletcher Knebel's article in the July 12, 1966 issue of *Look*. Knebel attributes his explanation to the three Commission lawyers and one of the autopsy doctors (apparently Dr. Boswell).

At the autopsy proper on November 22, 8-11 p.m., the doctors had not found an exit wound (or a bullet channel) and were puzzled. The next day they learned from Dr. Malcolm Perry of Parkland Hospital, Dallas, that there had been a bullet wound in the throat, obliterated by a tracheotomy operation. This led the doctors to conclude that the throat wound (which they never saw) was the exit wound. Their report was completed on November 24, and sent to the White House on the 25th. The Secret Service then received the report, and, according to statements published recently, sent it to the Commission on December 20 and to the FBI on December 23.

If this is what happened, it could account for the discrepancy between the FBI's first report and the autopsy report. But why didn't the
supposedly thorough FBI ask for the autopsy report or check with the
doctors? How could the FBI have conducted an effective investigation
without at least ascertaining the contents of the autopsy report? Is the
December 9th FBI report an accurate account of what the doctors
found from their one and only look at the body on November 22?

A most interesting document concerning this question has recently
come to light, discovered by a Mr. Paul Hoch in the papers in the National Archives (and published in full in Appendix I to this volume). It
is the report by two FBI agents, F. X. O'Neill and James W. Sibert, on
what happened at the autopsy. The report was dictated on November
26, 1963, based on what these two agents saw and heard while the doctors were examining President Kennedy on the night of November
22nd. (It may be of some significance that neither Sibert nor O'Neill
was ever called to testify before the Commission, and that the Commission did not think that their report was worth including in the
mass of documentation in the volumes of exhibits.) They list all of the
persons present and the number of photographs and X-rays taken of
the body. They state that during the latter stages of this autopsy, Dr.
Humes located an opening which appeared to be a bullet hole which
was below the shoulders and two inches to the right of the middle line
of the spinal column.

Then they describe Dr. Humes probing this opening with a finger,
and determining that the missile's trajectory was downward at 45-60
degrees, and that the bullet had gone in less than a finger length. No
bullet was found by X-rays, and no point of exit was discovered, so "the
individuals performing the autopsy were at a loss to explain why they
could find no bullets." At this point, the FBI report tells us that the
FBI men received word about the discovery of the whole bullet, No.
399, in Parkland Hospital, and that Dr. Humes was informed of this.
Dr. Humes immediately offered his opinion that this accounted for the
fact that the bullet "which [had] entered the back region," had not
been located, and that "it was entirely possible" that the bullet came
out on to the stretcher during cardiac massage in the hospital. This

account is quite consistent with those of Secret Service agents Kellerman and Greer, who were also present at the autopsy, although Kellerman attributes the statement that there was no exit to the back wound to Colonel Finck. Kellerman quotes Finck as saying, "There are no lanes for an outlet of this entry in this man's shoulder" (II: 93) and also as holding that No. 399 could have dropped out of the wound in Parkland Hospital.

The report of O'Neill and Sibert seems obviously to be the basis for the medical information in the December 9th and January 13th FBI reports. Almost the same words are used and none of the technical vocabulary of the autopsy report appears in any of these documents, indicating that the two major FBI reports were probably prepared without reference to the contents of the "final" medical report. With the corroboration of the Secret Service men, it would certainly seem that the O'Neill-Sibert document reflects, and reflects accurately, what was found and what was surmised at the autopsy on November 22nd. These witnesses all describe a back wound, not a neck wound, and also state that no path of exit was found, and that No. 399 falling out of the back seemed to be the only possible explanation of the data.

Then, if we accept Knebel's account, the doctors' findings were altered or revised the next day. On the morning of the 24th, Dr. Humes reports that he burned "certain preliminary draft notes" (II:373 and XVII:48). These may have been the findings of November 22nd, saying much the same as the O'Neill-Sibert account. Dr. Humes says the undated "official" autopsy report was drafted on November 24th, and that he finished it just as he heard that Oswald had been shot. Is this later report based solely on inferences from a wound the doctors never saw, but only heard described on the telephone by Dr. Perry? It would do much to help stem criticism and speculation if the doctors would frankly and publicly discuss what happened, and if they would offer an explanation for the discrepancy between the reports of the FBI men and Secret Service men who were present at the autopsy and the findings presented in the final version of the autopsy report.

In the August 1, 1966 issue of *Greater Philadelphia Magazine*, it is stated that Dr. Humes refuses to discuss the discrepancies. He is quoted as saying, "I'm not concerned with what was in the FBI report. We did our job and we signed the report and it was straightforward and unequivocal. We don't feel we should discuss the matter any more. That is the position we are taking and that is the position we have been instructed to take by our superiors" (p. 1). If this is the case, the public should demand to know what superiors are involved, and why they want to prevent any elucidation of these apparent contradictions.

In view of Knebel's explanation—which seems to be the one that the Commission staff and at least one of the autopsy surgeons want to stick to—it is interesting that Knebel also indicates that the final autopsy report may be wrong. "The doctors may well have erred in their autopsy finding." Erred concerning what? Perhaps concerning where the entrance wound was, or concerning the path of this first bullet? But just how or why they may have erred, and exactly when, remains a mystery that must be clarified. Their errors, if any, may be due to the fact that on Nov. 23rd, the doctors no longer had access to the X-rays and photographs. Hence, their deductions of the path of the bullet may have been based on inadequate data or on faulty memory. Knebel's explanation, which the FBI seems willing to underwrite, indicates a high degree of incompetence on the FBI's part.

The FBI says its first reports "were merely to chart a course and were not designed to be conclusive" (*Look*). Does that mean they were supposed to be inaccurate? They were prepared at the request of the President to get the basic facts, at a time when the FBI was the only official investigative agency dealing with the case. The reports were considered to be of "principal importance" by the Warren Commission when it started out. And how can the FBI explain that after receiving the autopsy report on December 23 it still issued a supplemental report on January 13, 1964, containing supposedly false information on the most substantive question: Where did the first bullet hit Kennedy and where did this bullet go?

The FBI has not as yet tried to explain why its report of January 13 contradicts the autopsy report. In the *Los Angeles Times* of May 30, 1966, Robert Donovan quotes an FBI spokesman as saying only that "the FBI was wrong when it said 'there was no point of exit.'"

"The FBI agents were not doctors, but were merely quoting doctors, the FBI spokesman said."

So it would seem that even when the FBI states bluntly that "X is
the case," this can be wrong, and only based on hearsay. This raises
the problem of determining when the FBI is reliable. (Was it when it
said Oswald was not an FBI agent?) How reliable are its many, many
reports, in the twenty-six volumes? When is the FBI to be taken at its
word? One can understand the willingness of all concerned to disavow
the FBI reports of December 13, 1963, and January 9, 1964. The texts
printed by Epstein hardly do credit to the FBI, since the reports are so
rhetorical and tendentious, and are bound to prove an embarrassment
now that they have been made public. But one would have assumed, or
hoped, that the facts given in these most important initial documents
in the investigation would have been correct.

Three

The Mystery of the Back Wound

If the FBI reports are false, is the Commission position then defensible, in view of the FBI photos of Kennedy's jacket and shirt published in Epstein's book? Its one-bullet theory depends in part on this bullet following approximately the path described in the sketch in the Commission Exhibit 385, entering the back of Kennedy's neck, and exiting at his throat on a downward path, then entering Connally's back and exiting below the nipple, going through his wrist, and finally reaching his femur (Commission Exhibits 679-80 and 689. See Appendix II). But if Kennedy was shot in the back, then there is something basically wrong with the very possibility of the Commission theory. Further indication that he was shot in the back is provided by Secret Service Agent Hill, who was sent in after the autopsy to be a witness as to where the wounds were located on the President's body. When he testified, he stated, "I saw an opening in the back about 6 inches 'below the neckline to the right-hand side of the spinal column" (II: 143). A bullet traveling downward would have exited from the chest, where there was no wound, and would have struck Connally at too low a point to inflict the damage. So the FBI pictures of the President's clothing become very significant, especially since the photos of the coat and the jacket shown in the Warren Commission's Exhibits 393 and 394 are so badly reproduced that it is not possible to see where the holes are, though they are clearly described by both Specter and Dr. Humes as being "approximately 6 inches" below the collar (II: 365). Some of the comments on Epstein's book by hostile critics who were associated with the Commission appear to concede that the FBI may have been right in locating the bullet in the back; and the FBI photographs definitely indicate that this was the case. Suggestions have appeared that Kennedy could have been bending over at the time, and so a bullet in his upper back could have exited from his throat (without hitting his chin??). But if this were so, the bullet would obviously have been too low to hit Connally where it did; and the Zapruder pictures clearly rule out the possibility that Kennedy was bending over at this time.

The *Detroit News*, June 5, 1966, p. 22A, offers another possibility, that Kennedy's coat was hiked up and bunched at the time. They offer a photo "taken just seconds before the first bullet." The issue is of course the condition of his clothes at that very moment. Zapruder's pictures don't show this; and they portray only a front view of Kennedy.. However, if the jacket was bunched, it seems most unlikely that a bullet fired at neck level would leave only one hole in the jacket nearly six inches from the top of the collar. And even if it were somehow possible, this would still leave the problem of the shirt. Would a buttoned shirt hike and bunch in this manner, that is, rise in such a way that a point nearly six inches below the top of the collar would at that moment be at neck level, and not be doubled over?

Dr. Humes tried to offer some possible explanations, although he had previously said that the holes in the clothing conform "quite well," and that "the wounds or the defects in 393 and 394 (the shirt and the jacket) coincide virtually exactly with one another" (II:366), which should place the wound well into the back rather than in the neck. First Dr. Humes somewhat disowned the diagram No. 385, prepared at his instructions: "385 is a schematic representation, and the photographs would be more accurate as to the precise location" (II:366). But the photographs, of course, have never been seen by the Commission, the FBI, nor the public, nor even, as it turns out, by Dr. Humes himself or by his fellow autopsy surgeons, since the undeveloped negatives were given to (not seized by, as Lane suggests) the Secret Service.

According to an article by Jacob Cohen in *The Nation* of July 11, several lawyers on the Commission staff stated in interviews that the photographs were "not published at Robert Kennedy's request," and Cohen speculates that if the Kennedy family "asked that this material be kept in the family, the Warren Commission might not have pressed to examine it"; it is not known whether or not the photos have ever, in fact, been developed, and hence seen by anyone.

Exhibit No. 385 was drawn, Humes said later on, to a certain extent from memory and to a certain extent from the written record (II:730). While indicating that No. 385 may not exactly represent the actual state of affairs, Dr. Humes also moved the clothing holes upwards by saying that the relation of the defects in the clothing to the wound on the body would depend upon how the clothes had hung on a person, and how that person was built physically. President Kennedy's muscular condition, he argued, would have pushed the clothes higher on his body. (One assumes, however, that Kennedy could afford to have bought suits that fitted him to begin with; and it has been reported that he wore custom-made shirts that presumably fitted well.)

Next Dr. Humes put forth the suggestion that Kennedy was raising his hand, and therefore was pulling his clothes still higher. All of this still seems insufficient to get a hole in the back to enter the neck. And, interestingly, Commission Exhibit No. 397 (XVII:45), an autopsy chart drawn up by Humes and Finck during the actual autopsy, shows the bullet well into the back, and not near the neck at all, a good six inches below the collar. But the measurements given on this chart locating the wound are identical with those Humes employed to describe a "low neck" wound (II: 361).

Arlen Specter's attempts to explain the difference between the FBI photographs and the Commission's report are no more convincing than Dr. Humes's. His statements on the matter in a recent interview with Joseph Fonzi in the *Greater Philadelphia* Magazine were confused and did not clarify matters:

"Well," said Specter, when asked about this in his City Hall office last month, "that difference is accounted for because the President was waving his arm." He got up from his desk and attempted to have his explanation demonstrated. "Wave your arm a few times," he said, "wave at the crowd. Well, see if the bullet goes in here, the jacket gets hunched up. If you take this point right here and then you strip the coat down, it comes out at a lower point. Well, not too much lower on your example, but the jacket rides up."

If the jacket were "hunched up," wouldn't there have been two holes as a result of the doubling over of the cloth?

"No, not necessarily. It ... it wouldn't be doubled over. When you sit in the car it could be doubled over at most any point, but the probabilities are that ... aaah ... that it gets ... that ... aah ... this ... this is about the way a jacket rides up. You sit back ... sit back now ... all right now ... if ... usually, I had it, where your jacket sits ... it's not ... it's not ... it but if you have a bullet hit you right about here, which is where I had it, where your jacket sits ... it's not ... it's not ... it ordinarily doesn't crease that far back."

What about the shirt?

"Same thing."

So there is no real inconsistency between the Commission's location of the wound and the holes in the clothing?

"No, not at all. That gave us a lot of concern. First time we lined up the shirt ... after all, we lined up the shirt ... and the hole in the shirt is right about, right about the knot of the tie, came right about here in a slit in the front ..."

But where did it go in the back?

"Well, the back hole, when the shirt is laid down, comes ... aah ... well, I forget exactly where it came, but it certainly wasn't higher, enough higher to ... aaah ... understand the ... aah ... the angle of decline which ..."

Was it lower? Was it lower than the slit in the front?

"Well, if you took the shirt without allowing for its being pulled up, that it would either have been in line or somewhat lower."

Somewhat lower?

"Perhaps. I ... I don't want to say because I don't really remember. I got to take a look at that shirt."

Even if one could somehow connect the holes in the jacket and the shirt with a wound in the neck (and I doubt it can be done), the original problem remains: the time interval on Zapruder's pictures between Kennedy's being wounded and Connally's being hit. As we have seen, the Commission has to hold to the theory that the Governor was hit at the same time as the President, but that his reaction was delayed. The pictures, however, definitely show him without noticeable reaction when Kennedy had already been struck. Connally's clear testimony is that he heard the first shot (and the bullet traveled much faster than the speed of sound), looked for its source to the right and to the left, and then was struck:

We had just made the turn, well, when I heard what I thought was a shot. I heard this noise, which I immediately took to be a rifle shot. I instinctively turned to my right because the sound appeared to come from over my right shoulder, so I turned to look back over my right shoulder, and I saw nothing unusual except just people in the crowd, but I was interested, because once I heard the shot in my own mind I identified it as a rifle shot, and I immediately—the only thought that crossed my mind was that this is an assassination attempt. So I looked, failing to see him, I was turning to look back over my left shoulder into the back seat, but I never got that far in my turn. I got about in the position I am in now facing you, looking a little bit to the left of center, and then I felt like someone had hit me in the back (IV: 132).

The Commission has to have Connally oblivious to the wounding for about a second, while he is looking, even though his fifth rib was smashed and his wrist shattered, and even though he stated positively that when hit he felt something slam into his back. Even Dr. Humes, who seems to be the apparent author of the one-bullet hypothesis and of the theory that Governor Connally had a delayed reaction to being shot, declared, "I am sure that he would have been aware that something happened to him" (II: 376). The problem of whether the Commission theory is at all possible first turns on whether Kennedy was hit in the neck or the back. The FBI and the Secret Service witnesses to the autopsy say that he was hit in the back; the final autopsy report and exhibit No. 385 put the wound in the neck. A couple of inches makes all the difference in whether the one-bullet hypothesis actually states a genuine possibility. A simple factual matter like this should be definitely ascertainable. But the Commission did not examine the photos or X-rays of the autopsy, and it remains unclear where these are now to be found. A report in the August 15 Newsweek stated that "the whereabouts of these photographs and X-rays remains one of Washington's most puzzling mysteries. A diligent two-month inquiry ... has failed to turn up a single government official who can, or will, give a simple answer to the question: 'Where are the Kennedy autopsy photos?'" The article by Jacob Cohen in *The Nation* discusses in detail the mysterious fact that none of the interested parties ever saw these data. Instead the Commission makes bullet No. 399 the key. If the bullet fell out of Connally after traversing the two victims, then the Commission could claim, in seventeenth-century theological style, that if it happened, it must be possible.

Four

The Strange Career of Bullet Number 399

Bullet No. 399 raises all sorts of problems. Medical experts in Dallas who had treated Governor Connally doubted that the same bullet had struck both the President and the Governor though they granted that it was theoretically possible. Two of the doctors who performed the autopsy on Kennedy held that No. 399 could not have done all of the damage to Governor Connally, let alone Kennedy.

Dr. Humes said it was "most unlikely" (II:375-6), and Dr. Finck said it could not have done this (II:382). Both based their view on the fact that there are too many fragments in both Connally's wrist and femur. Vincent Salandria, in *The Minority of One*, calculated that No. 399 may have lost only about 2.5 grains of its estimated original weight, while more than 3 grains of fragments were either still in Connally or had been recovered from his body. Some of the medical testimony concerning the fragments is contradictory, but Dr. Shaw, who operated on Governor Connally's chest, was clear in stating that "... the examination of the wrist both by X-ray and at the time of surgery showed some fragments of metal that make it difficult to believe that the same missile could have caused these two wounds. There seems to be more than three grains of metal missing ... in the wrist" (IV: 113). And Dr. Gregory, who minimized the weight of the fragments still in the wrist, admitted that the largest fragment or fragments—"the major one or ones"—had been lost; therefore they could not be measured or weighed (IV: 123).

It was not possible, in any case, to determine the exact original weight of bullet No. 399 before it was fired. In its present condition it weighs 158.6 grains. Similar 6.5 bullets had weights of around 160 and 161 grains. Since there are variations in weight among these bullets, Frazler testified that, "There did not necessarily have to be any weight loss to the bullet." Further, the only place that he could suggest where any material at all could have come off the bullet was at the base of it, which is slightly flattened (III: 430). Neither Frazier nor the doctors seemed to think that any material had come off the top part of the bullet. Second, other bullets shot from Oswald's rifle through any substance became mashed, unlike pristine No. 399, which is supposed to 'have gone through two human bodies, and have smashed Connally's rib, wrist, and entered his femur. Commission Exhibit 858 (XVII:851), a photograph taken during tests sponsored by the Commission, shows a bullet fired from Oswald's gun through a skull filled with gelatin. The bullet is quite distorted.

There is no evidence that the Commission could obtain anything like pristine No. 399 in any of its tests—except when it was trying to obtain bullets for comparison purposes, probably by firing into cotton wool, or some such material. Commission Exhibit No. 572 shows two nearly perfect bullets, obtained by FBI expert Robert Frazier for comparison with No. 399 and with the two fragments found in the car.

Incidentally, Specter's attempts to explain the undamaged condition of bullet No. 399 in the Greater Philadelphia Magazine are no more convincing than his comments on the FBI photos: How then had 399 emerged unscathed?

"The way the bullet went through the Governor's wrist," explains Specter, "it really tumbled through his wrist."

Were any tests made to determine the results of a bullet tumbling through a cadaver wrist?

"You can't fire a bullet to make it tumble," said Specter.

Wouldn't a tumbling bullet be more likely to be deformed than one hitting at a higher velocity on its streamlined nose?

"I think it was unusual for the bullet to come out in such perfect shape," Specter says, "but very plausible."

Did any of the test bullets come out in such shape?

"No."

Third, no one knows near whose stretcher No. 399 was found. Arlen Specter stated that there was evidence which would show that No. 399 was from Governor Connally's stretcher (II: 368 and 374). The Report emphatically states that "A nearly whole bullet was found on Gov. Connally's stretcher at Parkland Hospital after the assassination" (p. 79). It is only by tenuous inference that the Commission reached the conclusion that a Mr. Tomlinson took Governor Connally's stretcher off the elevator on the ground floor after the Governor had been taken to the second floor for surgery. Tomlinson says only that he found a stretcher on the elevator and removed it. Some time later on, No. 399 was discovered by Tomlinson when he adjusted two stretchers that were blocking the entrance to the men's room, one that he had removed from the elevator, and another that was standing in the corridor.

At this stage of our knowledge of the case, neither Mr. Tomlinson, nor anyone else, knows which stretcher the bullet came from, nor whose stretchers these were, nor whether either Kennedy or Connally was ever on either one of them. There is no real factual basis for the Commission's claim that the bullet was on Connally's stretcher. The FBI had earlier said it was Kennedy's stretcher. Tomlinson just did not know and refused to guess (VI:128-34). There were other patients in the hospital. The stretcher might have come from upstairs or might have come from the emergency section. The Commission did not really find out where the stretcher Tomlinson moved came from, so it has no evidence as to which stretchers may be at issue. It traced Kennedy's back to Trauma Room No. 2, and Connally's back to the elevator, but whether either of them is one of the stretchers Tomlinson handled nobody happens to know. Anyone could have entered the hospital. It was full of newsmen, spectators, Secret Service men, FBI men, and according to the management the place was a madhouse. There is even a report by a very reliable newsman, Seth Kantor of Scripps-Howard that Jack Ruby was there. This is denied by Ruby and strongly doubted by the Commission, though Kantor had serious corroboration of his claim in the form of his own notes plus the testimony of an eyewitness; and also Kantor knew Ruby well.

Fourth, when, late on November 22, the bullet was turned over to the FBI expert, Robert Frazier, in Washington, D.C., it didn't need any cleaning (III:428-29). "The bullet was clean and it was not necessary to change it in any way." Question by attorney Eisenberg: "There was no blood or similar material on the bullet when you received it?" Frazier: "Not any which would interfere with the examination, no sir. Now there may have been slight traces which could have been removed just in ordinary handling, but it wasn't necessary to actually clean blood or tissue off of the bullet."

Later on Frazier said that there was blood and some other material on the two smashed bullet fragments that were found in the Presidential car. The Commission lawyer, Eisenberg, apparently misunderstanding Frazier, said, "You mentioned that there was blood or some other substance on the bullet marked 399." Frazier, who had not said this, did not bother correcting Eisenberg, but just reported that no test was made of these materials (III:437). Weisberg makes a great fuss about all this, claiming that somebody must have cleaned bullet 399 earlier and thereby destroyed valuable evidence. However, the history of No. 399 does not indicate that anybody ever cleaned it that day, and thus that it may never have been dirty or soiled.

All of these points indicate not only that No. 399 can hardly have done the remarkable things the Commission claims it did, but that there is no evidence at all that it did these things, or came off Connally's stretcher, or ever was in Governor Connally's body. I will suggest presently an explanation for its features. At this point, I should only like to stress that No. 399 is a very shaky basis for the one-bullet hypothesis. To argue that it happened and therefore is possible is not persuasive here, since no one knows what had happened to No. 399 before it was found.

Five

The Failure of the Commission and the
Need for a Counter Theory

While the reasons for doubting the "official" theory are becoming much stronger, its ultimate defense is now crumbling because of Epstein's researches. If his account of how the Commission and its staff functioned is correct (and he seems to have the evidence), then the Commission did not do an adequate investigative job, and did not weigh all of the data carefully. It rushed through its work. The Commissioners and most of the staff were busy men who had insufficient time to devote to their task.

The Commission had no investigative staff of its own, and a few overworked lawyers in a very short time had to interview and check hundreds of witnesses. The Commission was inundated with so many FBI reports that no single person could master them. Pressure for a quick report made careful deliberation of the problems and issues almost impossible. Finally, the Report was written and rewritten in haste, with evidence marshaled, in a one-sided manner, to make a lawyer's brief for the "official" theory.

Then one staff member, Liebeler, wrote a twenty-six-page critique, showing many of the holes in this case, holes that would have given a lawyer for the defense a field day, and that have been the feeding ground for the critics.

Epstein's account no longer allows the high reputation of the Commissioners to make up for the deficiencies of the Report. After Epstein it will be hard to believe the Commission served the public well. Instead of ending all the rumors, they set the stage for a new and more serious era of speculations. They have damaged confidence in themselves and in any public body that might undertake to examine facts and possibilities about the death of President Kennedy.

But the critics have still failed to set forth evidence for a counter-theory in a systematic way. Weisberg does so only sporadically. "Of course the 'single bullet' theory is porous," The New York Times review of Epstein's book stated on July 3, "but no other explanation makes any sense." If we are to give up the official explanation, what can we put in its place? A two-assassin theory? A conspiracy? If so, what did happen? What role did Oswald play? How can the hard facts be accounted for? As Knebel quotes Allen Dulles, "If they've found another assassin, let them name names and produce their evidence."

Unfortunately one has mainly the twenty-six volumes of data to work with, and most of this was collected either in reference to the theory that Oswald was the lone assassin, or to buttress this theory. Material recently made available in the National Archives, some of which has already been used by Epstein, Salandria, Cohen and Lane, may prove to be a most important source. These materials include not only the originals of what is in the twenty-six volumes, but also apparently a good deal that the Commission did not see fit to include in its publication, such as the O'Neill-Sibert document, discussed earlier, and published here as Appendix I. I have not yet had the opportunity to see much of the data in the National Archives, and so can only theorize from the basic data of the Commission volumes.

Clues that might help speculation are few and far between. For instance, there are indications in the materials supplied by the Dallas Police that other suspects were arrested on November 22, 1963, but except for Molina, who was not involved, they are never identified. We learn that shortly before the assassination someone had an epileptic fit in front of the Book Depository, and that this caused much confusion and commotion. Right after the shooting, the Dallas Police rushed someone over to Parkland Hospital to find out about this. But we don't learn whether it was a diversion or a genuine illness, whether it was significant or a coincidence (XVII:465, XXII:599 and 601). A postage-due parcel arrived for the Oswalds in Irving on November 20 or 21, but we never found out what it is, and if it is a clue (XXIII:420). Who, besides the Paines, knew where the Oswalds lived at this time? Who might be sending them a package? Maybe it was a present for the baby, or maybe it was something they had ordered, or maybe it had something to do with the events to come.

At the present stage, any counter-explanation has to rest almost entirely on the material available in the twenty-six volumes and these are extremely difficult to work with. Fifteen of the volumes consist of testimony, depositions, and affidavits; eleven really bulky ones (around 900 pages apiece) contain documents and exhibits. The raw data appear in volumes XVI-XXVI. The documents are not properly indexed or identified. There is an index of witnesses who testified, of the names of documents—e.g., Shaneyfelt 6, Commission Exhibit 1215—and where they are introduced in the testimony, and volumes XXII-XXVI contain material not introduced, including some of the most important.

No index is given for the contents of the documents. Too often the documents are reproduced poorly, sometimes illegibly, sometimes incompletely, and sometimes redundantly. There is a bewildering collection of junk, as well as the most thorough kind of research of some points, and a great many discrepancies that are never explained or accounted for. Having been through the twenty-six volumes twice, I think enough discrepancies exist to provide the bare bones of a counter-theory based on two sorts of materials: first, evidence that some of the "official evidence" is not what it seems to be; and second, unexplained evidence suggesting that some sort of conspiracy involving or relating to Oswald existed as far back as Oswald's departure for Mexico, and was intensified from early November until at least November 22.

That something more was going on than the Commission believed is, I think, indicated by two crucial pieces of evidence, bullet No. 399 and the brown paper bag. Bullet No. 399 is distinctly odd and unusual. If it cannot have done the damage that occurred to Connally, what is it? It may have come from Kennedy's body if the FBI's report of what the doctors originally thought is true. But it has no signs even of being that. As the FBI expert said, "it wasn't necessary to actually clean blood or tissue off the bullet" (III: 428-29).

What other possibility is there? The Commission never seems to have considered the possibility that the bullet was planted. Yet in view of evidence concerning No. 399 it is an entirely reasonable hypothesis that the bullet had never been in a human body, and could have been placed on one of the stretchers. If this possibility had been considered, then the Commission might have realized that some of the evidence might be "fake" and could have been deliberately faked. Bullet No. 399 plays a most important role in the case, since it firmly links Oswald's rifle with the assassination. At the time when the planting could have been done, it was not known if any other ballistics evidence survived the shooting. But, certainly, the pristine bullet, definitely traceable to Oswald's Cacano, would have started a chase for and pursuit of Oswald if nothing else had, and would have made him a prime suspect.

Six

The Brown Paper Bag

Another piece of evidence that seems to be something different from what the Commission supposed is the brown paper bag found on the sixth floor of the Book Depository. This is the bag that, according to the Commission, was made by Oswald on the night of November 21-22 at Irving, and used by him to bring the rifle into the Book Depository. As Weisberg neatly shows (Whitewash, pp. 15-23), there are problems with all the information about the bag. First of all, both Marina Oswald and Wesley Frazier, who drove Oswald to Irving, report that he carried nothing with him when he went to Irving after work on the afternoon of the 21st (XXIV:408 and Marina's interview on November 23). When Frazier was interviewed on December 2, 1963, he said. "Oswald did not have a package and was not carrying anything with him at that time," that is, when they left the Book Depository (XXVI:348). The Commission was sufficiently worried about this point to recall Frazier and ask him if at some earlier time Oswald had paper with him, to which he answered, "No" (VII:531).

Next, the only two people who ever saw the bag, Frazier and his sister, Mrs. Randle, described a bag around 27-28 inches, whereas the found bag is 38 inches long. Both Frazier and his sister described it by referring to its position when Oswald carried it, its appearance, and where it was located in the car; all these gave results of around 27 inches. The longest part of Oswald's rifle, when disassembled, is 34.8 inches. Oswald is described as first carrying the bag with his arm down, and not dragging it on the ground; later he is said to have carried it cupped in his hand, and tucked in his armpit. "Oswald had this package under his right arm, one end of the package being under his armpit and the other end apparently held with his right fingers" (XXVI: 384).

Both descriptions are applicable only to a bag approximately 27 inches long. If Oswald, who was five foot nine, had carried a 38-inch bag cupped in his hand, it would have extended above his shoulder to ear level, a length that Frazier might have been expected to see and to remember. Despite serious efforts to get Frazier and his sister to change their estimate of the bag's size, they stood fast; and when one of them made a bag for the Commission that was supposed to approximate the original, it turned out to be about 27 inches long (XXI, V:408). The Commission nonetheless decided Frazier and his sister were correct about seeing Oswald with the bag, but incorrect in their description of it.

A further fact is that on the night of the 22nd, when Frazier first described the bag and estimated its size (about 2 feet), he was given a lie detector test which showed "conclusively that Wesley Frazier was truthful, and the facts stated by Frazier in his affidavit were true" (XXIV: 293). When Oswald entered the building, no one saw him with the bag. A Mr. Dougherty saw him enter and stated that he carried nothing, although a long bag should have been noticeable (VI:376-77). Dougherty was asked, "Do you recall him having anything in his hand?" to which he replied, "Well, I didn't see anything if he did." Later he was asked, "In other words, you would say positively he had nothing in his hands?" and he answered, "I would say that—yes, sir." Lane, in Rush to Judgment (p. 146), suggests that Oswald might have been holding the package in such a way that Dougherty couldn't see it. Oswald could also have thrown the bag into a trash-bin by the time he was seen by Dougherty.

The next thing reported by the Commission is that a bag 38 inches long was found near the notorious sixth-floor window. (In fact, it is never made quite clear exactly where this bag was found, and apparently no photograph was taken of it before it was picked up.) This bag was made from paper and gummed tape that were in the building. It has four very noticeable folds, but no indication of having been held on the top, as Frazier's sister saw it. It has one identifiable fingerprint and one identifiable palm print, both Oswald's. Also, as the FBI expert, Cadigan, testified, it contained no chemical or physical evidence of ever having contained a rifle. No oil or rifle debris, no distinctive marks of the rifle's location in it (IV:97). Asked to comment on the absence of marks, Cadigan said, "... if the gun was in the bag, perhaps it wasn't moved too much." But the Frazier-Randle descriptions show it had been moved a good deal. Besides being carried, it was bounced around on the back seat of Frazier's car.

The final problem, which only Weisberg seems to have noticed, is that, according to expert testimony, the found bag is put together with tape from the Book Depository's dispenser, cut by this machine. The machine operator, Mr. West (VI:356-63), indicated he was always at the machine and never saw Oswald use it. But, and this is crucial, tape could only be removed from and cut by the dispenser if it were wet. The FBI expert on paper, Cadigan, confirmed this when he testi-fied (IV :91). The tape came out of the dispenser dampened by a sponge. Oswald could only have gotten dry tape out of it by disman-tling the machine, but then it would not have been cut by the machine. So the conclusion seems to be that Oswald removed a wet piece of tape, three feet long. How could he have carried it to Irving and then used it to make a bag? If the machine-operator's description is correct, the bag would have to have been made in the Book Depository.

When? According to the Commission, on the 21st; and then Oswald returned it on the 22nd. But there would still be the conflict about its size between the found object and the testimony of the two observers. Weisberg presents all the discrepancies, but does not see what this can lead to except that the Commission's case is shaky. The only explana-tion, however, that seems to remove the conflict is that there were two bags, the one Frazier and Randle saw (which could have been a large supermarket bag) and the bag that was found. This could have been a deliberate effort on Oswald's part to sow confusion. The bag that was seen could have been disposed of just before Oswald entered the Book Depository (there are lots of rubbish bins at the back entrance, full of paper). Then, during the morning of the 22nd, the bag that was later found could have been manufactured to fit the dimensions of the gun. The bag was happily left in view near the alleged scene of the crime. A careful criminal could obviously have hidden it (along with the three shells). Its presence, like that of bullet No. 399, implicates Oswald. It has his prints and is large enough to have held the gun. Frazier and his sister can supply another link, and Oswald becomes the prime suspect.

If I am right that the bag that was found and the one that was seen are different, this means the rifle entered the Book Depository at a different time from Oswald's entrance on November 22, and that there was genuine premeditation in Oswald's actions, to the extent of fabricating evidence that would mislead the investigators. But, one might ask, if the gun was already in the building, why should Oswald bother fabricating a useless bag, and carry it to work that day, and, according to Frazier, claim that it contained curtain rods? It could well be that Oswald wanted to attract attention, get people to suspect him of activities that appeared to be related to the subsequent events of the assassination. What happened may have been intended to happen: Frazier and Randle told the authorities about the bag, and the authorities interpreted this as the means by which the gun got into the building. In this manner the investigators would have been misled, and would not look further to find out when and how the gun got to the Book Depository.

The bag and bullet No. 399 suggest that more was going on than the Commission recognized. There are many, many discrepancies in the evidence and in the Commission case. The critics have made much of these unanswered questions (and Weisberg's book is probably the best collection of them so far, though they are often stridently overstated). All of this, however, usually builds up to a big "So what?" since the critics still have not been able to present a reasonably plausible counter-explanation of what could have happened. Why, for example, should Oswald have tried to implicate himself as the assassin? I shall try to suggest why in what follows.

Seven

The Second Oswald

The twenty-six volumes contain numbers of strange episodes in which people report that they saw or dealt with Oswald under odd or suggestive circumstances: for example, that Oswald was seen at a rifle range hitting bull's eyes, that he and two Latin types tried to get financing for illegal activities from Mrs. Sylvia Odio; that Oswald tried to cash a check for $189 in Hutchinson's Grocery Store. These instances, and there are many of them, were dismissed by the Commission—though it continued to consider them up to the very end—principally on the grounds that they occurred when Oswald apparently was not there, or they involved activities Oswald reportedly did not engage in, such as driving a car.

Of course it is not uncommon for false reports of identification to turn up during a much publicized criminal investigation. However, in many of the cases ultimately dismissed by the Warren Commission, after much investigation and consideration, the witnesses seem reliable, and have no discernible reason for telling falsehoods so far as one can judge; they seem to be, in the Commission's overworked term, "credible." For example, Bogard, a car salesman, reported that on November 9, 1963, a customer came in to his showroom, gave his name as Lee Oswald (and, of course, looked exactly like the late Lee Harvey Oswald), went driving with him, and told him that he (Oswald) would come into a lot of money in a couple of weeks. Not only did Bogard have the corroboration of his fellow employees and an employee's wife, but he was also given a lie-detector test by the FBI. The FBI reported on February 24, 1964, that "the responses recorded were those normally expected of a person telling the truth" (XXVI: 577-78).

When the Commission had just about concluded its work, somebody still worried about this, so on September 1, 1964, the FBI was queried as to what questions Bogard had been asked when he underwent the lie-detector test. On September 19, 1964, the FBI replied, giving the questions and Bogard's answers. What they had asked amounted to an interrogation as to whether his story was true, whether Oswald had been his customer, and whether a photograph of Oswald portrayed his customer (XXVI:682). All one can say is that by normal standards of credibility, the FBI had established, both through finding corroborating witnesses and by its polygraph test, that Bogard was a credible witness.

Nevertheless, the Commission had satisfied itself from other testimony that (a) Oswald didn't drive, and (b) he spent November 9th in Irving, writing a strange letter to the Soviet Embassy. Cases such as the Bogard episode, varying in their degrees of confirmation and reliability, have attracted the attention of critics from the time of Leo Sauvage's article in *Commentary* in the Spring of 1964. They stirred rumors in the press from late November, 1963, onward. If these cases could not have actually involved Oswald and yet seem actually to have happened, then what? The Commission chose finally to dismiss them since Oswald could not have been the person in question. Leo Sauvage suggested someone was trying to imitate Oswald, that there was a second Oswald. Critics have brought up the second Oswald as an insufficiently explored phenomenon that might throw light on the case.

But why a duplicate Oswald? The Commission picture of Oswald is that of a pretty trivial individual of no significance until November 22, 1963. But the cases suggesting that duplication occurred begin at least as early as September 25, 1963, the day Oswald left for Mexico, when a second Oswald went into the office of the Selective Service Bureau in Austin, Texas, gave his name as Harvey Oswald, and wanted to discuss his dishonorable discharge. Yet Oswald at this time was riding a bus toward Mexico. (See Report, 731-33.)

Some have suggested that the point might have been to frame Oswald, but only a few instances of this kind seem to have any relevance to such a goal. I would suggest that the cases of apparent duplication can be classified in two distinct groups, according to the times when they took place. Rather than dismiss them, I suggest that it is more plausible to interpret them as evidence that Oswald was involved in some kind of conspiracy which culminated in the events of November 22, when the duplication played a vital role both in the assassination and the planned denouement, and may have been the reason for Tippit's death. Although the hypothesis of a second Oswald must necessarily be tentative and conjectural at this stage, I would suggest that it can resolve a large number of troubling problems concerning the assassination and provide a more plausible explanation of the case than that offered by the Commission.

If we turn to the data in a search for clues as to when Oswald might have started to get involved in affairs that might form some meaningful pattern, we find that the record compiled by the Commission indicates that as far back as Oswald's stay in New Orleans, some strange conspiratorial activities were going on. On the one hand, the correspondence of Marina Oswald and Ruth Paine indicates that Oswald was unhappy both because of his family life and his economic life, and wanted to return to Russia with his family.

On the other hand, from late May onward. Oswald started his pro-Castro activities, corresponded actively with the Fair Play for Cuba Committee in New York, the Communist Party, and the Socialist Workers Party, usually giving them false or misleading information about his activities. He spent a good part of his meager funds printing leaflets, membership applications and cards, etc., and hiring people to distribute literature. But, very significantly I think, he made no effort to change his FPCC Organization from a fiction into a reality. It never had any members except Oswald and the clearly fictitious "Alec J. Hidell"!

Mark Lane devotes Chapter 10 of *Rush to Judgment* to the problem of Hidell, and makes much of the fact that there was a Marine whom Oswald knew, John R. Heindel, who, in an affidavit, declared that "I was often referred to as 'Hidell'". Lane suggests that this is what Oswald may have called him and tries to show that the Commission did an inadequate job by purporting to demonstrate that Hidell was a fictitious person. However, the Hidell who plays a part in Oswald's life definitely seems to have been fictitious. A Sgt. Robert Hidell was given as a reference by Oswald in New Orleans around May 16, 1963 (XXII: 145). A Dr. A. J. Hideel (sic) is listed on Oswald's international vaccination form as having given Oswald a vaccination on June 8, 1963 (XVII:693). The name is printed with Oswald's equipment, and the doctor's address is P.O. Box 30016, New Orleans, whereas Oswald's Post Office box was No. 30061. A. J. Hidell appears as a name on various identification cards that Oswald had in his possession when he was arrested, including a Selective Service card which had Oswald's photo on it. The signature of A. J. Hidell on various documents is in Oswald's inimitable handwriting, including the order blank for the Carcano (XVII:677-8 and 681-3). Exhibit 819, Oswald's membership card in the New Orleans branch of the FPCC, is signed "A. J. Hidell" by Marina. All the checking by various investigative groups could turn up no Hidell who met the conditions of being a participant in Oswald's life in Dallas and New Orleans, and the data certainly makes it look as if Oswald was inventing a series of Hidells with various functions. Lane is, of course, right in saying that Sgt. Heindel was never asked whether he had played any part in Oswald's life. Heindel, incidentally, was from New Orleans. His affidavit, in fact, deals mainly with what a poor soldier Oswald was when he was stationed in Japan (VIII: 318).

In any case, Oswald made no effort to look for local leftists or to seek sympathizers for the FPCC, for instance at Tulane University, where he might have found them. The one person who came to see him, Marina says, he treated as an anti-Castroite plant. To confuse matters, Oswald even put the address of the anti-Castroites on some of his literature. Oswald lied to the FPCC, the police, and the FBI about his organization, claiming it had thirty-five members, that it met at people's homes, that he, Oswald, received telephone or postal instructions from Hidell.

These deceptive activities culminated in August 1963, with Oswald's visit to the anti-Castroites, Carlos Bringuier and friends, and his expression of interest in joining, and helping their para-military activities. In a few days he followed this with his distribution of FPCC literature near their headquarters, which caused a fight with them—they felt they had been betrayed by him. But according to the reports of the police and others, the fight was not a fight at all: Oswald simply put his arms down and told Bringuier (a former functionary under Batista) to hit him. Subsequently, Oswald pleaded guilty to disturbing the peace, when he was clearly innocent, and Bringuier pleaded innocent, when he had in fact struck the blow. In jail Oswald demanded to see the FBI, and tried to convince agent Quigley that he, Oswald, really was involved in pro-Castro activities. The arrest was followed by Oswald's appearance on radio and TV defending Cuba against Bringuier and others. Oswald sent distorted reports and clippings of his achievements to the FPCC, and, in an undated memorandum to himself, outlined all of the data he now had to show that he actually was a pro-Castro activist (XVI: 341-43).

This memorandum seems to have been designed for the Cuban Embassy in Mexico to convince them of his bona fides. But a problem remains—why, if Oswald was pro-Castro, and wanted to go to Cuba, didn't he organize real FPCC activities instead of fake ones? Why did he lie about and distort his accomplishments to the FPCC, the Communist Party, and apparently the Cuban Embassy? It is interesting that Oswald lied to almost everybody, whether friend or foe. In Russia, even from the outset, he put false information about his family on forms, false information that differed from form to form about his mother being dead, having no siblings, etc. (XVIII:427, for example). The memorandum suggests he wanted to fool the Cubans, since his organization of materials is deliberately misleading. Oswald last wrote to the FPCC on August 17, 1963, telling of all that had happened, and indicating that a good many people were now interested (on August 1, 1963, he had revealed that there were no members of his branch); that he had received many telephone calls (Oswald had no phone); and that he wanted lots of literature, especially about travel restrictions to Cuba (XX:530). The FPCC didn't hear from him again, but on September 1, 1963, both the Communist Party and the Socialist Workers Party heard from him that he was planning to move to Washington, Baltimore, or Philadelphia, and wanted to contact them there. But Oswald didn't write them again until November 1, 1963. As far as we can tell he wrote to no one until then.

Marina says Oswald had decided to go to Cuba via Mexico in August. The letters announcing his plans to move East may have been to mislead the FBI, if Oswald knew they were reading his mail, and his insistence on an interview with Quigley may have been to make sure that they were aware of his existence. Was Oswald really trying to get to Cuba and Russia through Mexico? The evidence suggests that he was not. He had earlier applied for a visa to go to Russia, and he had his new passport. On July 1, 1963, Oswald had asked the Russians to rush Marina's visa, but to treat his separately. He didn't write them again, as far as we know, until the letter of November 9th, though Marina had written on July 8th pressing her case. In August, the Russian Embassy had informed the Oswalds that the material had been sent to Moscow for processing, and Oswald made no effort to speed up the matter.

On September 22, 1963, he told Mrs. Paine's friend, Mrs. Kloepfer, that it usually takes six months to go to Russia (XXIII: 725). Then he apparently went to Mexico City a couple of days later, on September 25th, on a fifteen-day visa (not the six-month one that he might easily have obtained), visited the Cuban Embassy and asked for a transit visa to go to Russia via Cuba. By linking his trip to Cuba with a Russian voyage, he led the Cubans to call the Russian Embassy, who said the case would take months to handle. Oswald then became furious with the Cubans, not the Russians, and, according to Sylvia Duran of the Cuban Embassy, he claimed he was entitled to a visa because of his background, partisanship, and activities (XXV: 636). Any investigation of these probably would have led to his being turned down.

He said he needed a visa right away because his Mexican one was running out and he had to get to Russia immediately. He obviously could have gotten to Russia faster by traveling from New Orleans to Europe. The Russian Embassy apparently was not helpful and indicated it would take four months before anything was done. Though the Report (p. 735, note 1170, based on confidential information) says that Oswald came back to both the Cuban and Russian Embassies, there is no evidence that he really pressed his case. Señora Duran had given him her phone number, yet he doesn't seem to have used it. He doesn't seem to have known of or cared about the final disposition of his case by the Cubans a few weeks later. By linking his application for a Cuban visa to a Russian one, Oswald seems to have precluded any rapid action. If the Report is correct that Oswald had only $200 when he left New Orleans, he couldn't have gotten to Russia anyway. Oswald's dealings with Russian bureaucracy surely taught him, as his notes on Russia indicate, that quick action was most unlikely.

The abortive trip to Mexico seems to have involved a good many mysterious and as yet unexplained elements. The same could be said about Oswald's political activities in New Orleans during that summer. In both cases, however, there are signs of a similar sort of pattern. Oswald seems to have contrived to give people the impression that he was engaged in pro-Castro activities, and that he intended to travel to Cuba and Russia. His actual behavior was, however, in contradiction to these apparent aims in various respects; and his behavior in Mexico seems almost to have been designed to make sure that he could not succeed in his avowed aim of going to Cuba and Russia. Much remains to be clarified about Oswald's activities in New Orleans and Mexico, but from what we already know, these activities strongly suggest some sort of conspiratorial involvement.

Eight

The Two Oswalds in Texas

At the very same time that Oswald was in Mexico, a series of unusual events was occurring in Texas. On September 25, the visit of "Harvey Oswald" to the Selective Service in Austin (for 30 minutes) took place. The Report (p. 732) dismisses it because Oswald wasn't in Austin. Mrs. Lee Dannelly, the Assistant Chief of the Administrative Division, interviewed this purported Oswald, and on November 24, 1963, before she knew that it couldn't have been Lee Harvey Oswald, told her boss in great detail what had taken place in this meeting.

She described how Oswald had told her that he was registered in Florida, and was living in Fort Worth, how he was having difficulties in employment because of his discharge from the Marines, etc. Mrs. Dannelly, like most of the others who saw the second Oswald, definitely identified Oswald as the person she had dealt with from his photograph (XXIV: 729-34).

A Texas newspaper editor, Ronnie Dugger, said that Mrs. Dannelly is reliable (XXIV:736). Her account is also somewhat confirmed by reports that Oswald was seen that day in a car in Austin by a printer and a waitress (XXIV:734. 73(5. 740, and 743). On the evening of September 25, a Mrs. Twiford of Houston received a phone call from

Oswald between 7 and 9 P.M. Oswald could not have been in Houston then, according to all known means of surface transportation that were then available to him (he doesn't seem to have traveled by air either), yet it appeared to be a local call. Oswald claimed he wanted to see Mr. Twiford, the Socialist Labor Party leader for Texas, before flying to Mexico (XXIV:726 and XXV:4-5). This may have been Oswald, calling long distance, though why, if he was planning to defect to Cuba, he should care to see Twiford is a mystery. Could it have been the second Oswald creating mystifying data about Oswald's whereabouts?

On September 26, the striking incident involving Mrs. Sylvia Odio is supposed to have occurred. Mrs. Odio, a Cuban refugee leader in Dallas, reported to the Commission that she and her sister were visited by two Latins and one "Leon Oswald," who claimed they had come from New Orleans, were about to leave on a trip, and wanted backing for some violent activities. Then, and in a phone call the next day, Mrs. Odio was told more about Leon Oswald by one of the Latins called Leopoldo: The next day Leopoldo called me... then he said, "What do you think of the American?" And I said, "I don't think anything."

And he said, "You know our idea is to introduce him to the underground in Cuba, because he is great, he is kind of nuts ... He told us we don't have any guts, you Cubans, because President Kennedy should have been assassinated after the Bay of Pigs, and some Cubans should have done that ... And he said, "It is so easy to do it." He has told us (XI: 372).

She was also told that Oswald had been in the Marine Corps and was an excellent shot. When Mrs. Odio heard of the assassination, she was sure these men were involved. When she saw Oswald's picture, she knew! (XI:367-89). When Mrs. Odio testified, attorney Liebeler asked her, "Well, do you have any doubts in your mind after looking at these pictures that the man in your apartment was the same man as Lee Harvey Oswald?" to which she immediately replied, "I don't have any doubts." (See Appendix III). The Commission made sporadic attempts to discount Mrs. Odio's story, though she had the corroboration of her sister who was present when the three gentlemen called upon Mrs. Odio, but they kept finding that Mrs. Odio was a quite reliable person, sure of what she had reported. Finally, Manuel Ray, the leftist anti-Castro leader, gave her a testimonial and said she would not have made up the story nor have had delusions; Cisneros, the former leader of JURE, said she was reliable (XXVI:838-39). The only conflicting evidence was that of a Mrs. Connell, who said Mrs. Odio had told her she had previously known Oswald and that he had spoken to anti-Castro groups, which if true would indicate that Oswald had been more involved with anti-Castro elements in the Dallas area than Mrs. Odio admitted.

In August, 1964, the Commission apparently became concerned about the Odio episode, thinking it might really indicate a conspiracy. On August 28, 1964, Rankin, the Commission's chief counsel, wrote J. Edgar Hoover, "It is a matter of some importance to the Commission that Mrs. Odio's allegations either be proved or disproved" (XXVI: 595. See Appendix IV). The Commission had figured out that Oswald actually had enough time to leave New Orleans, come to Dallas and meet Mrs. Odio, then go on to Houston and Mexico, though this seemed very unlikely. It was probably with great relief that they received the FBI report of September 21, 1964. (See Appendix V.) This stated that on September 16 the FBI had located one member of the group that had visited Mrs. Odio and he had denied Oswald had been there, but had given the names of the other two, one of whom was a man "similar in appearance to Lee Harvey Oswald." The FBI said it was continuing research into the matter and "The results of our inquiries in this regard will be promptly furnished to you" (XXVI:834-35).

The Commission seems to have been satisfied that it had established that Oswald had not visited Mrs. Odio, and did not care that it appeared to have also established a strong possibility that there was a double for Oswald, that is, a man who looked like him and may have used his name. One would have expected that, if the Commission had really been interested in clearing up all of the questions and rumors about the case, it would have stopped everything, located this

man and the other two, found out if he had been masquerading as
Oswald, and, if so, why. Weisberg uses this as crucial evidence that
the Commission had established a conspiracy, and subsequently
ignored it. But Epstein shows that by September 21, the mad rush to
publish the Report was so great that this took precedence over
anything else.

The FBI report does appear to support Mrs. Odio's account that a
meeting took place. One wonders then, gnawingly, what did they find
out next? Was the man "similar in appearance" acting as a double for
Oswald? Did he use Oswald's name? What was he involved in when he
went to see Mrs. Odio? Was he connected with the other double-
Oswald episodes?

This matter remained in the dark until very recently. Lane, in his
Rush to Judgment, pp. 340-42, reports on some of the subsequent developments, based on material that has come to light in the National
Archives. These documents, (Commission Document No. 1553), were
sent to the Commission by the FBI on November 9, 1964, long after
the Report had appeared. (See Appendix VI.) Right after obtaining the
testimony of Mrs. Loren Hall about the meeting with Mrs. Odio, the
FBI checked with the other alleged participants, both of whom denied
ever having met Mrs. Odio.

Both also denied having been in Dallas together. Mrs. Odio was
shown photographs of all of the parties, as well as photos of some others who had been involved with this group. Both she and her sister
stated that none of the individuals seemed to be the ones they had
seen, with the possible exception of one who looked something like
"Leopoldo." In fact, by the time J. Edgar Hoover sent his letter concerning the matter to the Commission on September 21, 1964, the FBI
had pretty well discredited its report, which Hoover was passing on to
the Commission.

Lane does not discuss some interesting new information in the FBI
documents. They show that all of the people involved with Hall were
engaged in anti-Castro paramilitary activities, and the purpose of
their trips to Dallas (there were at least two, in September and
October, 1963), was to get financing and equipment for a military

venture against Cuba. The accounts, which do not always agree, indicate that at least some of this group visited another Cuban refugee in the same group of apartments where Mrs. Odio lived, and Hall originally thought he and some of the others had met her. In October, 1963, Hall and another man were even arrested in Dallas for possessing dangerous drugs and were interrogated by various intelligence services.

If the FBI findings in Commission Document No. 1553 finally suggest that these were not the people involved in the Odio incident, then who was? (One report, dated October 2, 1964, states without comment or further explanation that Mrs. Odio "had attempted suicide during the last week.") Were there other anti-Castro groups in Dallas at the time, or was there some group pretending to be anti-Castro in order to introduce Mrs. Odio to the second Oswald? Since the evidence, including that in the later FBI reports, shows that Mrs. Odio is considered quite reliable by almost everyone who knows her, then who did visit her on September 26, 1963, and why did they do so? (Also, why did the FBI not correct its report of September 21, when they already knew it to be questionable, and why did they let the Commission finish off its Report under the possibly mistaken impression that the participants in the Odio affair had been found, and did not include the real Lee Harvey Oswald?)

The Odio episode strongly indicated that duplication and conspiratorial activities involving Oswald were going on; and indeed the possibility remains open that Mrs. Odio was visited by Oswald himself, since the FBI's later findings do not preclude this. Two items connected with Oswald's return from Mexico to Dallas seem further suggestive. A Mexican bus roster shows the name "Oswald," written in a different hand from the other names. It is known that Oswald was not on that bus, yet no satisfactory answer was ever found for his name being put on the roster, though it apparently happened after the trip on October 2 (XXII: 155; XXIV:620; XXV:578 and XXV:852).

On October 4, when Oswald was back in Dallas, the manager of radio station KPOY in Alice, Texas, reported that Oswald, his wife, and small child visited him for twenty-five minutes, arriving in a battered 1953 car. The Report diligently points out that (a) Oswald didn't drive, and (b) he could not have been in Alice at that time (Report, p. 666). The incident is the first of several in which it appears that Oswald and his family may have been duplicated. Instead of seeing it as part of a possibly significant pattern and considering it further, the Commission was satisfied once Oswald had been disassociated, from the event.

In October there seems to have been little double-Oswald activity. This may be explained by the facts that Oswald was looking for a job at the time and that his second daughter was born on October 20. But a second group of incidents can be traced from early November until November 22, almost all in the Dallas-Irving area. (Irving is the Dallas suburb where Marina lived with Mrs. Paine.) These begin to occur at about the same time as Oswald's resumption of conspiratorial activities. Having settled down in Mrs. Johnson's rooming house and having obtained a job, Oswald attended two meetings, one on October 23 to hear General Walker, the other on October 25, a meeting of the ACLU, at which he spoke up and criticized Walker, and told one person after the meeting that John F. Kennedy "is doing a real fine job, a real good job" (IX:465). The housekeeper at Mrs. Johnson's, Earlene Roberts, said that Oswald never went out in the evenings. She was obviously mistaken (VI:437 and 442).

On November 1, Oswald rented a Post Office box and listed as users the FPCC plus, of all things, the ACLU. (Was he getting ready to set up a fake branch of that organization for some dark purpose?) On the same date he wrote and posted a letter to Arnold Johnson of the Communist Party in New York. This was an airmail letter which was delivered, incidentally, after Oswald was dead, and which is almost entirely devoid of Oswald's usual misspellings. In it he asked for advice on infiltrating and agitating within the ACLU (XX: 271-73). He also explained to Johnson that he had changed his summer plans to move East, and that he had now settled in Dallas. On November 4, he joined the ACLU and asked its national office how he could get in touch with "ACLU groups in my area" (XVII:673), although he had attended a meeting, knew well that Michael Paine was a member, and, in the November 1, 1963, letter to the Communist leader, Johnson, had stated when and where the ACLU meetings were regularly held in Dallas.

On November 6th or 7th, another interesting episode occurred. Someone looking like Oswald, of course, came into a furniture store in Irving, Texas, looking for a part for a gun. (The store had a sign indicating it was also a gun shop.) This person then went out and got his wife and two infants out of a car, returned, and looked at furniture for a while. The children turned out to be exactly the ages of the Oswald children. Two people saw and talked to this Oswald and later identified him and Marina as the people in question. (When Marina was confronted by these witnesses, she insisted she had never seen them before, though they stuck to their story.) The "Oswalds" then drove off, after getting directions as to where to find, a gun shop (XXII: 524, 534-36, 546-49). This may well have been the day an Oswald took a gun into the Irving Sports Shop, right near by, an episode that occurred in early November.

A clerk in the shop found a receipt on November 23 that he had made to a man named Oswald for drilling three holes in a rifle. Yet Oswald's rifle had two holes and they were drilled before Oswald got the gun. An anonymous caller told the FBI about this episode on November 24 (so as to make sure it was known?). The receipt seems genuine; the clerk is sure he ran into Oswald somewhere, and the clerk seems reliable. His boss was convinced, but the Commission dismissed the case since there was no evidence that Oswald owned a second rifle (XXII: 525 and 531; XI:224-40, 245753). Incidentally, all other Oswalds in the Dallas-Fort Worth area were checked, and it was found that none of them was the Oswald who had had his gun repaired.

November 8 seems to have been a crucial day in the development of whatever conspiratorial activities Oswald and the second Oswald were up to. The Report blandly states that "the following Friday, November 8, Oswald as usual drove to the Paine house with Frazier" (p. 740), but there is no evidence for this. The footnote reference is to

Wesley Frazier's testimony, where he says nothing of the kind. And Marina has unequivocally stated that Oswald did not come home on November 8, that he claimed he was looking for another job, and that he came to Irving around 9 A.M. on the 9th, without explaining how he got there (XXIII: 804). (This is a not-untypical example of the sloppy documentation in the Report, in which potentially interesting leads were overlooked.)

On November 8, two marked cases of double Oswaldism took place in Irving, Texas. A grocer, Hutchinson, reported that on that day Oswald came in to cash a check for $189, payable to Harvey Oswald (XXVI: 178-79 and X: 327-40). He claimed that Oswald subsequently came to the store once or twice a week in the early morning and always bought a gallon of milk and cinnamon rolls, items that Oswald probably would not have purchased, according to Mrs. Paine and Marina. Such an event as the attempt to cash a check is no doubt memorable and, as Marina wondered, where would Oswald get $189?

Also, a barber, right near the grocer, reported Oswald came into his shop on the 8th with a fourteen-year-old boy, and they both made leftist remarks. The barber said Oswald had been in his shop on previous occasions—although it seems most unlikely that Oswald could have been in Irving at any of these times—and had indicated he had been in Mexico (X: 309-27). The barber had even seen Oswald driving, and going with Marina into the grocery store, though the real Marina insists she was never in the store. And, of course, both the barber and the grocer immediately identified the photos of Oswald as their customer. The Commission dismisses all these reports on grounds that Oswald could not have been present or that they are denied by Marina.

The second Oswald became more active on the 9th. Except for a trip with Mrs. Paine to attempt to get a learner's permit for driving a car, the real Oswald spent the day at the Paine house writing a letter to the Russian Embassy strongly implying he was a Russian agent. (See Appendix. VII.) The letter was probably unintelligible to them, in that it referred to all sorts of events they presumably knew nothing about. It also contained a good many false statements concerning a conversation with FBI agent Hosty that probably never took place. Oswald thought the letter important enough to draft by hand, and then to type (XVI:33 and 443), a unique event, since Oswald always sent anybody and everybody handwritten, misspelled documents. He then left the draft lying around, partly exposed, and made no effort to rush his letter off. It is post-marked November 12th. Mrs. Paine saw it, was startled by what it contained, and made a copy to show the FBI (III: 13-17).

The FBI intercepted it, and its report on the matter showed no interest at all in Oswald's statements portraying himself as a man who had used a false name in Mexico, had "business" with the Soviet Embassy in Havana, and had been threatened by the "notorious FBI" for pro-Castro activities. The FBI report concluded that Oswald's letter merely indicated he wanted a Russian visa (XVII: 803).

While Oswald was writing his strange letter, two second Oswald cases occurred. One was the Bogard incident, which I have already mentioned, when an Oswald tested a car, driving over 70 miles per hour, dropped hints about receiving lots of money in a couple of weeks, and told the credit manager that if he were not given credit, he would go back to Russia and buy a car (XXVI : 450-452, 664, 684-85, 687 and 702-03).

This memorable performance at the Lord-Lincoln agency was coupled with one of the first appearances of a second Oswald at a rifle range. (There are indications of an earlier appearance during his Mexico trip.) From November 9th onward someone who looked just like Oswald was noticed at the Sports Dome Range, by several witnesses, always at times when the real Oswald could not have been there, either because he was at work, or was with his family. The second Oswald was an excellent shot, who did a number of things to attract attention to himself, firing odd weapons (some of whose descriptions fit Oswald's rifle), shooting at other people's targets, etc.

The Commission was impressed by the fact (Report, p. 318) that several witnesses, who seemed to be reliable, all gave similar descriptions of the man whom they saw, and of the kind of weapon that was being employed. Some of these witnesses had ample opportunity to observe the man in question. Malcolm Price, a friend of the owner of the rifle range, adjusted the scope on the man's weapon, and talked to him on one occasion, and saw him hit bull's-eyes (X: 370-72).

Garland Slack, a contractor and real estate developer, talked to "Oswald" on November 10th, and had an altercation with him on November 17th, when "Oswald" shot at Slack's target (X: 380). A dentist, Homer Wood, and his son were shooting next to "Oswald." "Oswald" was firing an odd weapon from which "a ball of fire" came out of the barrel each time it was used, and the marksman was shooting mostly bull's-eyes. Dr. Wood's son talked briefly to "Oswald" and identified his rifle as an Italian 6.5 carbine. Both Dr. Wood and his son independently recognized Oswald as the man they had seen at the rifle range.

The Report (p. 318), in evaluating these and other reports, said that in view of the number of witnesses and the similarity of their descriptions and reports, "there is reason to believe that these witnesses did see the same person at the firing range." But the Report goes on to insist that "there was other evidence which prevented the Commission from reaching the conclusion that Lee Harvey Oswald was the person these witnesses saw" (p. 319). Among the evidence offered is that Oswald could not have been there. He was in Mexico City when Price reported having seen him. He was in the Paine house and in his rooming house when Slack is supposed to have run into him. Some of the witnesses said they saw Oswald driving a car, which he did not do. The weapon reported being fired by "Oswald" differed in some respects from Oswald's Carcano.

For all of these and some other reasons, the Commission decided that it was not Oswald who was seen on the rifle range. But it could well have been second Oswald getting ready for his role in the assassination. I saw some of these rifle range witnesses being interviewed on television just after the Report was issued, and they still insisted that they had seen Oswald.

From November 12, the end of a long holiday weekend, until November 21, Oswald himself did not go to Irving. The weekend of the 16th and 17th he was reported to be at his room almost all of the time.

He worked every week day. We know of no letters he wrote during this period, and of no extra-curricular activities at all. But a second Oswald is reported on November 13, at the grocery store in Irving with Marina; and on the rifle range on the 16th, 171h, 20th, and 21st.

The only information about Oswald's own activities is from merchants in his Beckley Street area in Dallas: he went to a grocery (one also used by Jack Ruby); he made calls (apparently long distance) at a gas station (XXVI: 250); he was in a laundromat at midnight on the 20th or 21st (if the latter, it has to be second Oswald again); he took coffee at the Dobbs House restaurant on North Beckley in the early morning. One very suggestive sign of a second Oswald is a report by Mary Dowling, a waitress (XXVI: 516), that he had come into the Dobbs House on November 20 at 10 A.M. (when the real Oswald was at work) and had become very nasty about the way his order of eggs was prepared. (See Appendix VIII.) At this time, Officer J. D. Tippit was there "as was his habit" each morning at this hour, and glowered at Oswald. The FBI, in this report, rather than being excited at this sign that Oswald and Tippit had encountered each other before November 22, merely commented that Oswald was reported to have worked from 8:00 until 4:45 on November 20. They also showed no interest in why Tippit stopped on North Beckley each morning when it was not in his district or near his home.

Another possible clue about Oswald or second Oswald is that the Secret Service thought Oswald was responsible for ordering the anti-Kennedy "Wanted for Treason" leaflets, distributed in Dallas on November 21. The Secret Service pointed out that the copy had Oswald's typical spelling errors and that the person who ordered them around November 14 resembled Oswald, except for his hair (XXV: 657).

The next major, and final, report of the second Oswald's appearance is right after the assassination. One eyewitness to the shooting from the Book Depository, J. R. Worrell, saw a part of a gun sticking out of the building, heard four shots (and he is one of the few who heard four, rather than three), and ran behind the building. He there saw a man come rushing out of the back of the building, and run around it in the opposite direction. According to a Dallas policeman, K.

L. Anderton, Worrell told him that when he saw Oswald's picture on TV, "he recognized him as the man he saw run from the building" (XXIV: 294). It is an interesting indication of the Commission's concern in clearing up mysteries in the case, that when Worrell testified, all he was asked about this episode is whether he told the FBI the man looked like Oswald. Worrell said he didn't know (II: 201). He was not asked if the man did in fact look like Oswald, which he had told Anderton.

The final appearance of the second Oswald was also reported by Deputy Sheriff Roger Craig, one of the most efficient policemen at the scene of the crime that day. (See Appendix IX.) Craig heard one shot, followed by two others, and like so many others of the Sheriff's men at that time, he ran immediately up to the knoll and then to the railroad yards looking for the assassin. When he came back down to the area where Kennedy was shot, he ran into one of the puzzling witnesses, Rowland, who, according to Craig, told him that he had seen two men in windows on the sixth floor of the Book Depository before the shooting, one of whom was holding a gun with a sight. After talking to Rowland, Craig looked for the place where the bullet that missed the Presidential car had struck. About fifteen minutes after the shooting, he heard a whistle, and next saw a man run down from the Book Depository to the freeway, where he got in a light-colored Rambler station wagon, and then was driven away. Deputy Sheriff Craig tried to stop the car, but failed.

Much later that day, around 5 P.M., after taking part in the search of the Book Depository, he telephoned in a report of what he had seen, and he was asked to come down to police headquarters and to look at the suspect that they had in custody. He immediately and positively identified Oswald as the man he had seen get into the station wagon and be driven away (VI: 260-73, XIX: 524, XXIII: 817 and XXIV: 23). Sic transit Oswaldus secundus.

Craig saw Oswald in Captain Fritz's office, and reported that Oswald made several remarks. When asked about the station wagon, he said it belonged to Mrs. Paine, and that she had nothing to do with the matter. Then, after Craig identified him, Oswald said cryptically,

"Everyone will know who I am now" (VI: 270). When Craig testified on April 1, 1964, he was asked if he felt that the man he saw in Captain Fritz's office was the same man he had seen running towards the station wagon; he replied, "I still feel strongly that it was the same person" (VI: 273).

The Warren Commission dismissed all these incidents as mistaken identifications since they couldn't have been Oswald. The Commission treated Craig's case very gingerly. Although Craig may have seen someone enter a station wagon 15 minutes after the assassination, the person he saw was not Lee Harvey Oswald, who was far removed from the building at that time (Report, p. 253). There are more cases than I have mentioned here. Some are dubious, some possible. I have also heard of some cases that are not in the twenty-six volumes but seem quite startling and important. I noticed only one place in the twenty-six volumes where the conception of a second Oswald occurred to the Commission. One gets the impression that the hard-pressed staff found it convenient to ascribe all the incidents to tricks of memory and other aberrations, notwithstanding the fact that many witnesses were apparently reliable and disinterested people whose testimony was confirmed by others. Furthermore, they must have had considerable conviction to persist with their stories in the face of questioning by the FBI and Commission lawyers. The evidence seems to me compelling that there was a second Oswald, that his presence was being forced on people's notice, and that he played a role on November 22, 1963.

It is interesting, and may well be significant that the groupings of double Oswald occurrences can be correlated rather closely with news reports of Kennedy's plans to come to Dallas and of his route through the city. Fred Graham correctly states in the *New York Times* of August 28th that "Oswald got his job at the School Book Depository on October 15th, a month before anybody knew there would be a Presidential motorcade." But the Report tells us that the *Dallas Times-Herald* of September 13th stated that Kennedy was to visit Dallas; that both Dallas papers on September 26th (the date of the Odio episode) confirmed Kennedy's plan to visit the city and indicated the event would take place on either November 21 or November 22

(Report, p. 40). Thereafter there was much comment about Kennedy's impending visit in the papers, especially after the violent incidents that occurred during Adlai Stevenson's visit on October 24th. On November 8th (when second Oswald was seen in the grocery store and the barbershop, and when real Oswald's location is not known) the plans for the visit were confirmed in the newspaper.

The Report also points out that the traditional parade route is down Main Street, which anyone could have figured out would bring Kennedy within one block of the Book Depository; after Main Street, the procession was to go on to the Trade Mart. This route was mentioned in the *Dallas Times-Herald* on November 16th, and a detailed plan of the route, including the fateful turn onto Houston and Elm, appeared in both papers on the 19th. Thus, the second Oswald might have been planning his moves on the basis of the information about the Kennedy visit that he found in the press. We don't know how well informed Oswald was about the President's visit. Oswald apparently read other people's newspapers in the lunchroom at the Book Depository, often a day later. When his wife asked him on the 21st where the parade was going to be, he professed no knowledge of the subject.

Nine

The Assassination

If we take at face value the cases in which people saw someone who looked like Oswald, used Oswald's name, imitated Oswald's life and family, then how are they to be explained? I suggest that the duplication played a crucial part in the events of November 22. Second Oswald was an excellent shot, real Oswald was not. Real Oswald's role was to be the prime suspect chased by the police, while second Oswald, one of the assassins, could vanish as Worrell and Craig saw him do. If the crime is reconstructed in this way, most of the puzzles and discrepancies can be more plausibly explained.

Oswald, the methodical conspirator, goes to Irving on November 21, carrying nothing. He returns on November 22 with a package, about 27 inches long, attracting the attention of Frazier and his sister. The package vanishes by the time he enters the building. Oswald and second Oswald arrive separately. Since Oswald doesn't talk much to people, second Oswald can easily enter undetected. Previously, or that day, one of them has brought the gun into the building. How? Two intriguing details suggest that this may not have been the case.

These have been a problem. First, according to Marina, when Oswald went off to shoot General Walker, he left without the rifle and returned without it. He had secreted it in advance and afterwards. So he may have known how to do this. Second, a day or two before the assassination, someone had brought two rifles into the building, and Mr. Truly, the manager of the Book Depository, was playing with one of them, aiming it out a window (VII: 380-82). None of the employees mentioned this in their testimony, and it only came to the attention of the Commission because of a report that Oswald had mentioned it in one of his interrogation sessions. The other employees just had not noticed. In Dallas, guns are so common that on any day except the 22nd of November one could probably have carried one anywhere.

Oswald makes the bag that was later found. As we have seen, the only witnesses who saw the original bag were both adamant and cogent in insisting that it was not large enough to have held the gun; and the only witness who saw Oswald enter the building denied he carried a bag at all. By making a larger bag, Oswald creates an important, if confusing, clue. It connects him with the crime, helps to make him the prime suspect. At some time Oswald and second Oswald move several boxes to the sixth-floor window, either to establish another clue, or to make arrangements for the shooting, or both. (There is a set of still unidentified prints on the boxes [XXVI: 799-800], and all of the employees, police, and FBI who touched them have been eliminated.) Oswald seems to have spent a very normal morning at the Book Depository, and was seen working on various floors. He asked someone which way the parade was coming, as if to indicate that he was hardly concerned. Around noon Oswald told people he was going to have lunch. After that the next we know of him is that right after the shooting he was seen in the lunchroom, in complete calm, about to buy some soda pop.

At 12:30 or 12:31, the shooting began and was of extreme accuracy, far beyond anything the Commission could achieve in its tests with Oswald's rifle. Many of those present in the immediate area thought that the first shot at least came from the knoll area beyond the Book Depository. Some even saw smoke from this area (even though the Report claims there is no credible evidence of shots from any place except the Book Depository. It depends on what one considers credible). So, in keeping with the evidence, let us suppose that at least one shot came from the knoll. This might account for the throat wound that looked like an entrance wound to the Dallas doctors. Some others apparently came from the Book Depository. If these include Kennedy's back wound, Connally's wounds, and Kennedy's fatal wounds, the marksman was magnificent at hitting moving targets.

It should be stated that there is a problem for those, like myself, who doubt the "official" version of the shooting in accounting for what became of the bullets. If Kennedy was hit from in front in the throat, where did that bullet exit? If the first bullet entered his back and did not exit, what became of this bullet? If the bullet that injured Connally ended up in his femur, where is it? As yet I know of no satisfactory answers to these questions, unless the bullets fragmented or were deflected and disappeared in the confusion of that day.

The Commission, of course, has a neat solution in its theory about bullet No. 399, since this bullet is supposed to be the one that did everything—entered Kennedy's neck, caused the throat wound, wounded Governor Connally, and fell out of his body to be found in Parkland Hospital. But this explanation of the shooting only works if the Commission's general theory is possible, that is, if Kennedy were shot in the neck and not in the back; if the first bullet really went through his body; and if No. 399 could in fact have inflicted so much damage, and yet emerged in such pristine condition. And if this could be shown the Commission would still have created other problems to solve.

The critics at the present time have a genuine difficulty in offering an explanation that will accord with the scattered and incomplete bits of available data. The FBI expert, Frazier, was careful to leave open the possibility that a bullet could have been deflected on striking the President and "may have exited from the car" (V: 173). And two witnesses believed they had seen a bullet hit the pavement near the Presidential car, Mrs. Baker (VII: 508-09) and Mr. Skelton (VI: 238). But it may well be that at this stage of our understanding of the affair, no completely consistent account of all of the basic details can yet be given.

It so happens that Oswald's rifle could not be aimed accurately, and may not have been used at all. Strange as it may seem, no one ever checked to see if Oswald's rifle had been used that day, and no one reported the smell of gunpowder on the sixth floor. Deputy Sheriff Mooney, the man who discovered the shells near the sixth-floor window in the Book Depository, was specifically asked by Senator Cooper, "Was there any odor in the area when you first got there?" He replied, "I didn't particularly notice any," and also said that he did not smell any powder (III: 289). The three shells found near the window are odd in that the FBI reported they had markings indicating they had been loaded twice, and possibly loaded once in another gun (XXVI: 449). Weisberg has some very interesting and intriguing discussions about this, about the boxes and the conflicting information about their arrangement, and about the positions from which the shooting could have been done from the Book Depository window, all indicating that the event could not have taken place as surmised by the Warren Commission.

Weisberg suggests as a possibility, based on the information about the shell cases that J. Edgar Hoover sent the Commission (XXVI: 449-50), that the shells might have been fired from another gun, and then placed in Oswald's in order to connect them with his rifle. As for the boxes, Weisberg shows there is no clear picture or statement as to how they were arranged when found, and thus there is no way of telling whether they would have helped or hindered in the shooting. And there is a problem, depending on how far the window was open at the time, as to the position an assassin would have had to assume in order to fire from there. (See Weisberg's chapters 4 and 5.)

Also, some of those who saw a second Oswald at the shooting range reported that he collected the ejected shells after they flew out, and put them away. (The FBI accumulated all the 6.5 shells they could find in the Dallas area, and none was from Oswald's gun [XXVI: 600].) Certainly, if the marksman wanted to avoid detection, he would have collected the shells. If he had wanted Oswald's gun implicated, he would have left them where they fell. It is an interesting point that no evidence turned up indicating that anyone, anywhere, sold Oswald ammunition. The very few in Dallas who handled these shells had not, to their knowledge, dealt with him (XXVI: 62-64). The rifle was not sold to him with any ammunition. And, as Weisberg stresses, no rifle shells were found in his possession, or in his effects. If second Oswald did the shooting, he could have had additional shells. A confederate could have bought them in Dallas or elsewhere.

There is a report that Oswald bought ammunition in Fort Worth on November 2 (XXIV: 704), but Oswald was in Irving that day. According to an FBI report dated April 30, 1964, a Mr. Dewey C. Bradford saw Oswald in a gun shop in Fort Worth making the purchase, and Oswald told Bradford he had been in the Marine Corps. Bradford's story was corroborated by his brother-in-law. This may have been another appearance of second Oswald. But there is no indication that Oswald ever had any rifle ammunition (the shell fired at General Walker was unidentifiable).

Further, there were no identifiable fingerprints on the surface of the rifle, on the shells, or on the remaining bullet in Oswald's rifle (though there were, apparently, a few ridges that might be from fingerprints on parts of the gun). The famous palm print was old, and on a part of the rifle only exposed when disassembled. According to the Commission, this rifle had to be assembled that day, loaded with four bullets, fired rapidly, and hidden, without any fingerprints appearing on it. If they were wiped away by Oswald, when and with what?

According to the Commission's time schedule, he had barely enough time to hide the gun and get downstairs. If he loaded and fired while wearing gloves, where are the gloves? Second Oswald solves these problems. He could have wiped everything or worn gloves, since we have no inventory of his effects, and he had ample time. The palm print shows that Oswald at some time handled the rifle. Nothing shows who handled it on November 22, 1963, the most interesting day in the rifle's career.

Another point of some interest is the connection between the ballistics evidence and Oswald's rifle. The shells had been in Oswald's gun. Bullet No. 399, the one found in Parkland Hospital, had been in Oswald's gun. The mashed fragments (Commission Exhibits 567 and

569, XVII: 256-57) don't match up too well with comparison bullets in Exhibits 568 and 570.

To make the identification, the ballistics expert had to infer how the pictures would match if the fragments had not been distorted. Only good old No. 399 really matches up (Commission Exhibit 566, XVII: 255). Bullets fired from Oswald's rifle into anything seem to mash and shatter very easily. Were it not for the marvelous discovery of No. 399, there might have been quite a job connecting Oswald's gun with the remains after the firing.

Ten

After the Shooting: The Tippit Affair

After the shooting, what happened? According to my theory there were two assassins, plus Oswald, the suspect. Assassin one was on the knoll; assassin two, second Oswald, was on the sixth floor of the Book Depository. In spite of all the eye- and ear-witnesses who heard shooting from the knoll and saw smoke there, what I believe has kept reasonable people from believing anyone shot from there, besides the pompous denials of the Warren Commission, is that the sheriff's men and the police swarmed into and over this area immediately and found nothing. Anyone holding a counter-theory to the Warren Commission's, and accepting the evidence of at least one shot from the knoll, is obliged to give some explanation of how this might have occurred unobserved.

When I visited the scene of the crime, the ideal place for the shot to have come from seemed to be the parking lot on the top of the knoll. It has a picket fence, perfect for resting a gun upon. It can't be seen from the overpass. A shot or shots fired from there would get the right angles to conform to some of the medical evidence and the pictures. Then what became of the gunman? I submit he either put the gun in the trunk of a car and joined the throng looking for an assassin, or he,

plus gun, got into the trunk of a car. Cars were moving out of the
parking lot very soon after the shooting. Unfortunately, for
simplicity's sake, this requires two additional accomplices, one a
shooter and one a driver. But it provides an easy way for someone to
disappear from the scene right after the firing.

Some corroboration of this possibility recently appeared in the
Philadelphia Inquirer of June 27, 1966, in an interview with Mr. S. M.
Holland, who had previously reported seeing smoke rise from the knoll
area at the time of the shooting:

Backed up against the [picket] fence, says Holland, were a station
wagon and a sedan. The ground was muddy and ... there were two
muddy marks on the bumper of the station wagon, as if someone had
stood there to look over the fence. The footprints led to the sedan and
ended.

"I've often wondered," says Holland, "if a man could have climbed
into the trunk of that car and pulled the lid shut on himself, then
someone else have driven it away later."

As to the two Oswalds, we know that one, probably Lee Harvey,
was seen on the second floor at about a minute-and-a-half after the
shooting, by Policeman Baker and Mr. Truly. One, described with different clothes, was seen by an employee, Mrs. Reid, a few moments
later holding a coke and moving in the direction of the front exit.
Oswald Two left by the rear (observed by Worrell), hid until his ride
arrived, raced down to the freeway (observed by Deputy Sheriff Craig),
was picked up, and disappeared.

The real Oswald went on a strange journey, leaving a wide trail,
taking a bus from several blocks away (and taking a transfer he didn't
need), exiting from the bus a few minutes later, walking to the railroad station, and taking a cab. If he had really wanted to vanish
rather than be followed, he had ample opportunity to disappear into
the mob in downtown Dallas, to take a train, to go to the movies, or
anything. At the railroad station, he was in no great hurry. He even
offered a lady his cab.

According to the cab driver, Mr. Walley, an elderly lady came up
just as he was about to drive off with Oswald, and she wanted a cab.

Oswald "opened the door a little like he was going to get out and he said, 'I will let you have this one,' and she said, 'No, the driver can call me one'" (II: 256). Oswald insisted on riding in front with the driver (so he could be seen, perhaps), got off a few blocks from his rooming house, and walked there—another indication of his lack of haste. He rushed into the house, went into his room, and emerged a few minutes later.

Mrs. Earlene Roberts, the housekeeper, reported two interesting facts: one, that while Oswald was in his room (around 1 P.M.), a police car pulled up in front of the house and honked, waited a bit, and then drove off; the other that when Oswald left, he stood by the bus stop in front of the house (the bus that stopped there went back to downtown Dallas) for "several minutes" (XXII: 160 and XXVI: 165). In an affidavit dated December 5, 1963, Mrs. Roberts said that she looked out a moment after Oswald left, and that she does not know how long he stood there. When she testified before the Commission, she seemed to be confused on various matters. She was not, however, asked anything about this particular item.

Oswald claimed he went to his room to change clothes and to get his revolver. One of the many oddities of that amazing day is that when Oswald was arrested he had on him a payroll stub from the American Bakery Co. dated August 1960, a period when Oswald was in Russia. The stub turned out to have nothing to do with Oswald, but to belong to someone else who lived at the same address where Oswald once had lived. Maybe Oswald was collecting misleading data in case he was arrested. [XXII: 178 and XXVI: 542].) He then apparently walked to the place where the encounter with policeman Tippit occurred. The physical evidence about the times involved indicates it just might barely be possible for Oswald to have made this odyssey.

The Tippit affair is puzzling. It seems out of keeping with Oswald's calm, unflappable character that he would have shot Tippit on the spur of the moment. It seems odd that Tippit would have stopped a suspect. He was unimaginative, and had shown no real initiative in all his years on the force, as evidenced by his failure to get a promotion in thirteen years. It is hard to believe that, on the basis of a vague

description which must have fitted at least several thousand males in
Dallas that day, Tippit would have stopped Oswald far away from the
scene of the crime. Few other suspects were stopped in all of Dallas,
although the city contained thousands of white males aged thirty, five
foot nine, weighing around 165 pounds, a description that doesn't fit
Oswald, who was twenty-four and weighed much less.

The legal evidence that Oswald shot Tippit is pretty bad, and a
good defense lawyer might have prevented a conviction. The only witness to the shooting itself was Mrs. Markham, whose testimony was
strongly doubted by some of the Commission lawyers. Mark Lane has
done much to undermine the probative value of Mrs. Markham's evidence. The tape recording of his conversation with her (XX: 576-77, for
instance) does not inspire confidence in the reliability of her reports,
nor does her testimony to the Commission.

Many of the others who were in the area where the Tippit shooting
occurred, and who identified Oswald as being on the scene had already
seen pictures of him in the press or on television. The cartridge cases
found at the scene came from Oswald's pistol but could not be linked to
the bullets in Tippit's body, since the bullets were smaller than the revolver barrel and did not show identifiable markings. It is also odd
that the bullets found in Tippit and the recovered shells do not form a
matching set. Also there are conflicting reports from those present as
to what took place, as well as many other unsettled problems. Weisberg, Lane, and Sauvage have presented most of the difficulties.

None of the witnesses could offer any explanation for what happened. If Oswald did the shooting, as I am inclined to believe, what
could be the reason? If Tippit was suspicious of Oswald, Oswald had
all sorts of fake (A. J. Hidell) identification on him to satisfy the non-
too-bright Tippit. If Oswald was trying to disappear, shooting Tippit in
broad daylight would hardly seem to be a way of accomplishing that.

I should like to suggest an explanation of the Tippit affair with
reference to some of the above points. If Oswald's role was to become
the prime suspect, he did his job well. Within an hour he had become
the principal person sought by the police, independent of the Tippit
murder. If this was a conspiracy, and Oswald had his role qua suspect,

how was he to get away? The two assassins are rescued right away. Oswald goes off on his own to his rooming house. Just then a police car arrives. What better get-away than a police car, fake or real? As it happens, the Report mentions the fact that old Dallas police cars had been sold to private individuals. Oswald misses his ride, looks for it at the bus stop, and then starts up the street looking for it. Tippit comes along slowly. Oswald thinks it is his ride, and approaches the car. Tippit has had a confrontation with second Oswald at the Dobbs House on November 20, and recognizes him from the previous encounter. A monumental misunderstanding then occurs, and Oswald may suddenly have feared that Tippit realized what had been going on. Hence, the shooting. Oswald then disappears for half an hour, and mysteriously reappears across the street from the Texas Theatre. Because he didn't buy a ticket, he attracts attention and gets arrested.

The only other crucial event in this early post-assassination period was the finding of bullet No. 399. As I have already indicated, bullet No. 399 was essential in connecting Oswald's gun with the assassination. If it was never fired through a human body, then someone had to take it to Parkland Hospital and plant it. The descriptions of the chaos in the hospital indicate that almost anyone could have walked in and placed the bullet where it was found.

One conspirator could have left bullet No. 399 on a bloody stretcher, trusting it was Kennedy's or Connally's. Bullet No. 399 would again lead to making Oswald a suspect. The various clues—the shells, the brown paper bag, Oswald's prints on the boxes, the rifle, bullet No. 399, Oswald's absence from the Book Depository—would all lead a mammoth police search for Oswald, while the others could vanish. The conflicting data, due to the two Oswalds, would confuse the search. Oswald presumably had some get-away planned, so that he, too, would disappear.

Then, possibly, as Fidel Castro suggested in his analysis of November 29, 1963, all of Oswald's fake Cuban activities would lead to cries that Oswald had fled to Cuba (XXVI: 433). Castro, in fact, offered a very interesting and intriguing commentary on the affair in this speech, pointing out some of the oddities and implausibilities in the initially reported data. He also indicated that he was suspicious of Oswald's pro-Cuban activities, and thought they were a planned cover to create the illusion that Oswald was on Castro's side. When the deed was done, and Oswald "left a trail, was identified, and disappeared, they would then say he came to Cuba." Castro also indicated in this speech that Oswald had "passed through Cuba" when he went to Russia, which doesn't seem possible in view of the data gathered about the trip.

The Tippit affair and the arrest in the movie theater are all that went awry. If I am right that the Tippit affair was an accident, it also led to the arrest by getting a large group of policemen into the area searching for Oswald. Only if he wanted to be arrested can I believe that the Tippit shooting was deliberate. It certainly would make it harder, if not impossible, for Oswald ever to get released from jail.

If Oswald's role was to attract all suspicion, while not being an actual assassin, his behavior in prison certainly fits this. Marina claimed at one point that he wanted a page in history. If so, and if he had done it, he would have gained lasting fame and shame by proclaiming his achievements. Instead he calmly insisted on his innocence, and contended that as soon as he got his lawyer it would be established. The police, the FBI, and the Secret Service were all amazed by his sangfroid and his continual protestations of innocence. His brother Robert tells us that Lee assured him of his innocence and told him not to believe the "so-called evidence" (XVI: 900). Oswald also insisted that the famous photograph showing him holding the rifle was a fake, and that he, with his photographic experience, knew how it was done.

If the plot was as I have suggested, Oswald played his role well. The police chased him and found him, and ignored all other clues, suspects, and possibilities. The second Oswald data would probably have made all eyewitness evidence against Oswald useless. (Somebody did go to the trouble of making sure that the FBI knew about a second Oswald by calling on November 24th and telling them about the tag in the Irving Sports Shop.) Except for the Tippit episode, Oswald's subsequent arrest and Jack Ruby's shooting, it might have been a perfect plot. Nobody could place Oswald at the scene of the crime. (What is

Brennan's poor testimony worth, especially if there was a second Oswald?)

The paper bag would have been worthless as a clue, especially if two bags were introduced. Oswald may well have waited in the lunchroom until Baker and Truly turned up, and then thought he had a solid alibi. The planted evidence of a second Oswald's movements would have raised reasonable doubts, by showing that another reconstruction of the crime was and is possible.

Eleven

The Remaining Questions

My reconstruction is, of course, no more than a possibility, but unlike the Commission's theory, it fits much of the known data, and requires fewer miracles or highly unlikely events. Since the second Oswald was an excellent shot, my theory makes the skillful marksmanship plausible. By having two assassins, this theory fits the testimony of the majority of the observers that at least the first shot came from the knoll.

The theory does not require the dismissal of all of the people who saw second Oswald as mistaken, no matter how much corroboration they have. The theory accounts for bullet No. 399 and its role, and it offers some explanation for the Tippit affair.

The Commission resorts to extremes to make the one-assassin theory possible, and has had to select some of the weakest evidence and weakest witnesses in order to hold on to its conclusion. Its time reconstruction really shows how improbable it is that Oswald did it all, all by himself. And the Commission is left with all sorts of discrepancies: the absence of Oswald's fingerprints on the gun surface and the bullets; the absence of rifle ammunition; the unaccountable behavior of Oswald if he had done it; any serious account of motivation, etc. The criticisms of Cook, Epstein, Lane, Salandria, and Weisberg leave the Commission with the problem of defending just the bare possibility that their theory could hold up.

The answers to Epstein that have appeared are simply concerned to show that the one-bullet hypothesis is possible (it never was probable), and so far they haven't done a good job of it. If Kennedy was shot in the back, and some replies to Epstein tend to concede this point, then it seems unlikely that anything can redeem a one-assassin theory. In this connection, one point must be made clear: The Commission's Report made no attempt to resolve the contradiction between the FBI reports and the autopsy. The O'Neill-Sibert report clearly strengthens the reliability of the FBI reports of December 9, 1963, and January 13, 1964, as accurate accounts of where the first bullet entered the body and of how far it penetrated. The Commission apparently chose to ignore the matter, and to keep the conflicting FBI data out of public view by omitting all of this material from the reams of documents published in the twenty-six volumes.

The question whether the FBI reports were accurate can only be answered if the photographs of the autopsy and the X-rays are made available for examination by responsible and independent observers, if not by the public at large. Since the Commission's theory of a single assassin depends heavily on this point, the photos and X-rays should be made available immediately. Cohen, in his article in The Nation, while professing to support the Commission's theory, has stressed the need for some responsible examinations of these materials.

Sinister accusations have been made, and the longer these X-rays and photos are hidden, the more credible these accusations will appear. If there is something sinister afoot, let us expose it. If there is not, let us silence these accusations and also inhibit what promises to be decades of dreary fantasizing (p. 49).

I do not know how dreary or how fantastic the speculating will be, but if it turns out that the photos show that the bullet hole is in Kennedy's back, and the X-rays show that the bullet did not exit from the body, then there should be an urgent public demand for an accounting of what has gone on. If the photos and the X-rays confirm the critics' view, then there will have to be some explanation from the Commission and the doctors for the information they have set forth.

From the beginning of the investigation a two-assassin theory was a more probable explanation for all of the strange events of that day. The evidence collected, however, left few traces of a second assassin, but many problems in proving that Oswald was one of the killers or the only one. As I have argued, the problem can be overcome by admitting a conspiracy theory suggested by the "evidence" of the brown paper bag and bullet No. 399. But to establish the exact nature of a conspiracy would obviously require a lot more data than are available in the twenty-six volumes since the Commission didn't look into this possibility. What I have outlined is a tentative version that seems to fit the data available at present. Further investigation may produce different explanations of some of the incidents I have mentioned. Other and better hypotheses can probably be set forth if more information becomes available.

The political or social nature of the conspiracy must be purely speculative at this stage. We know too much about Oswald (but still not enough to ascertain what he was really up to), and nothing about the others. Perhaps, as someone has suggested to me, Oswald was a minor figure in the venture and his proclivities in no way represent those of the group. Maybe Oswald met some far-right extremist when he went to hear General Walker on October 23. Maybe some right-wing Cubans involved him in a plot when he was in New Orleans, or maybe he got involved with some leftist plotters in New Orleans, Mexico City, or Dallas.

Whatever information might emerge from a renewed investigation, a reading of the twenty-six volumes forces one to the conclusion that the Commission did a poor job; it served the American and the world public badly. But Weisberg's constant charge that the Commission was malevolent is, I believe, quite unfounded. Until Epstein came along, one searched for some possible explanation for the deficiencies of the Dallas Police, the FBI, and the Commission. Epstein has at least explained the failings of the last group. They did a rush job, a slap-dash one, defending a politically acceptable explanation.

The American Press, as well as others in positions of responsibility, would not and could not dream of a conspiratorial explanation. In a world in which conspiracies are going on all of the time—in business (the anti-trust cases), in crime (the Mafia), in foreign affairs (the CIA)—it somehow was still not imaginable that two or more persons could decide to assassinate the President of the United States. The activities of Weissman (the far-right-winger who put the ad in the paper) show that a conspiracy to defame the President was going on in Dallas among a handful of rightists. Why was this possible, but not a conspiracy by others to shoot Kennedy? The printer, Surrey, refused to reveal who was conspiring to pass out leaflets denouncing the President. The information gathered about this clearly indicated that some group was involved, probably another far-right one.

If the answer is, So what? there are lots of conspiracies going on, but not in this particular case, then I would argue that a two-assassin theory makes the most (and maybe the only) sense. And so, in this case, if we are ever to understand what happened, we have to consider seriously all of the indications that there was a conspiracy in which second Oswald played a part.

The assassination of Kennedy was a momentous event in our history. We cannot hide from it by clinging to a hope that one lonely, alienated nut did it all by himself, and that nobody else was involved. And we cannot hide from the fact that some of our most serious and well-meaning citizens have catered to our childish needs for security, and have given us an inadequate and perhaps grossly misleading explanation of the event. Many of us in this country are afraid to face reality, and part of our reality is living with our history. Can we continue to live a lie about what happened in Dallas on November 22, 1963, or has the time come to face what it means and what it involves for all of us? The public must cry out for a real examination and understanding of the events of that day.

Epilogue

This small book began as a review of Epstein's and Weisberg's books, and in its first form was written in June 1966. Its present form dates from the summer of the same year, and includes some material brought forth in Mark Lane's *Rush to Judgment*. In the few months since I originally stated my views on the subject of Kennedy's assassination, the whole atmosphere of the discussion has changed considerably, especially in the United States. As of last spring, the critics were mainly amateur sleuths and speculators, disregarded by the "serious" press. Occasionally the public would be reminded by an article by Leo Sauvage or Vincent Salandria that there were doubts as to whether the official theory of the Warren Commission was the final word on the matter, but by-and-large, not much attention was paid to the subject, and the public seemed satisfied that the Warren Commission had done its duty, and that the case, except for some loose ends, had been solved.

It was Epstein's findings, I believe, that really changed all of this, and his questions, reinforced by those of Lane, Sauvage, Weisberg and myself, have led to a radically new situation, in which articles, reviews, debates, comments, are appearing everywhere. It is no longer a handful of critics and amateur sleuths who are alone calling for a reopening of the investigation of Kennedy's death. The results of a Harris poll published in the United States in late September 1966 showed that a majority of the American public now doubted the Warren Commission's explanation. Moreover, serious publications and important persons have been asking for a reinvestigation or a reopening of the investigation, and indications have appeared that at least some unofficial investigations will now take place.

For example, Professor J. W. Liebeler of UCLA, who was a staff lawyer on the Warren Commission, has stated his intention to conduct such an inquiry with the assistance of his students. A story appeared in *Newsweek* saying that an American foundation is anxious to finance a new investigation. A New York Congressman, Theodore Kupferman, has introduced a resolution in Congress asking for a new inquiry. Whatever comes of these projects, I think it is now evident that the work of the Warren Commission has failed to quiet the fears and rumors, and has proven inadequate to provide a lasting explanation of the events of November 22-24, 1963, in Dallas.

The early attempts to dismiss Epstein and the other critics have failed. Millions of people have read our books, or read about them in magazines and newspapers, and have shown genuine concern. The Commission staff has begun to feel the need to argue with the critics, and to try to explain the points at issue. Two of the staff, Messrs. Griffin and Liebeler, have appeared in debates with various of the critics, including myself. Arlen Specter, the District Attorney of Philadelphia, and one of the authors of the one-bullet hypothesis, has given a fifteen-page interview to *U.S. News and World Report* (October 10, 1966).

A few others, like Curtis Crawford of *New York*, have tried to defend various aspects of the Commission's case against our criticisms. (See, for instance, his answer to me in the *New York Review of Books*, October 6, 1966.) *The New York Times* has lamented the fact that it now seems difficult to find defenders of the Warren Commission, and it is easy to find opponents and critics. It seems that the present atmosphere will only be, and can only be, clarified by a new investigation. Many major faults of the Commission's work have become evident, so that even such defenders, as Judge Fein in the *Saturday Review* (October 22, 1966), concede pretty glaring weaknesses in the procedure and results. It is clearly not possible to recreate the serene atmosphere (pre-Epstein) through argument with critics of the report. Stony silence certainly will not work. And I, like many others, feel that only a new investigation can lead to any general acceptance of a view as to what happened in Dallas three years ago.

I believe that the affair has now become something between a legal problem and an historical one, and what is most needed is an investigation by both lawyers and historians to evaluate the evidence, for we are not just concerned about whether a court of law would have convicted Lee Harvey Oswald of murdering either or both John F. Kennedy and J. D. Tippit. We are also, and probably more concerned about what the historical judgment will be as to the role of Oswald in the affair.

Many people who were never convicted have been adjudged guilty on the basis of the historical record, and many who were convicted have been later adjudged innocent. The case of Oswald cannot be a court case, but it definitely is an historical problem. As a recent issue of *Ramparts* points out, there are a great many facts and documents in the case that are not in the public domain, and that are not yet available for serious study and evaluation; and there are definite indications of attempts to prevent some from coming to light (as suggested by the material of Penn Jones, in his *Forgive My Grief*, and of *Ramparts* dealing with the intimidation and the startling death rate of witnesses).

What I feel is needed now is an investigation independent of the U.S. government, since it is obviously a party to the dispute in view of the fact that governmental agencies and individuals were involved in the production of the Warren Commission Report. It is hard to conceive of a governmental group that could or would challenge the Chief Justice and the FBI, or could or would be willing to investigate and evaluate their conduct in regard to the inquiry into Kennedy's assassination. An investigatory group would have to start with the alleged discrepancies raised by the critics.

To perform a genuine historical service, it would have to be willing to consider these points on their merits, and not as challenges to the

Warren Commission Report that have to be answered and/or dismissed. The aim of a new investigation, needless to say, should be to
arrive at answers and solutions that reasonable men will accept as the
best in terms of the evidence available. Many reasonable men now
have doubts about the accuracy of the autopsy report in its location of
the wound from the first bullet, about the one-bullet hypothesis, about
the role and history of bullet 399, and a number of other matters. In
view of this, the investigatory body should have the power to call such
witnesses as Dr. Humes, Arlen Specter, and J. Edgar Hoover, and to
have access to all the material now in the National Archives, plus the
still missing autopsy photographs and X-rays.

This new investigatory body should be composed of full-time working members who can really take the time to analyze materials, and
look into problems. Probably most important, it should include at least
one of the critics to satisfy everyone that the present points at issue
are thoroughly considered. (A lot of later troubles might have been
avoided if the Commission had taken Mark Lane more seriously, and
not treated him as a hostile witness and a nuisance, as well as if the
Commission had called Leo Sauvage as a witness when he was raising
his early critical points.) To construct, finance and operate such an investigation should not be an insurmountable problem. American foun-
dations can probably provide the monetary resources. Some body of
concerned, public-spirited citizens could create the investigatory body,
and public opinion demanding a new and more thorough investigation
may be able to provide the prestige and power.

Since Epstein's book appeared, a kind of haphazard new
investigation has been going on, mainly in terms of newspaper
interviewing and questioning (much of which should have been done
long ago). In retrospect I think we can now see that Epstein posed a
new sort of problem. First, and perhaps most significant of all that his
book accomplished, it severely damaged the prestige of the
Commission, and destroyed the myth that it had been completely
objective, thorough and definitive.

The prestige of its members and its staff could not make up for the
defects Epstein revealed in its operations. The information he set

forth, supplied in good part by Liebeler, made it difficult if not impossible to believe that the Commission Report settled matters for good, and that its members had really sifted and settled all the problems. Second, Epstein revealed the glaring discrepancy between the official autopsy report and the FBI reports of December 9, 1963, and January 13, 1964, on the location and path of the first bullet to hit Kennedy (a matter which is crucial to the one-bullet hypothesis).

This discrepancy was not apparent in the Report or the 26 volumes, since these original FBI reports were not published, nor was the matter discussed, even when taking testimony from the autopsy surgeons. The later discovery of the Sibert-O'Neill FBI report of November 26, 1963 (reprinted in this book) makes the discrepancy more forceful, since we seem to have an eye-witness account of the autopsy that directly conflicts with the official findings (though it is consistent with the testimony of the Secret Service agents who were present, with Commission Exhibit 397, drawn at the time by Dr. Humes, and with the holes in Kennedy's clothes). There is also another Sibert-O'Neill report, dated November 29, 1963, that has turned up, but I have not yet seen it.

This material has led defenders, principally Messrs. Griffin, Liebeler and Specter of the Commission staff, to try to construct satisfactory explanations. These constitute at least a beginning for a new investigation. I have only heard Griffin's and Liebeler's answers orally (in a debate with them in New York on September 30, 1966), and since I have no transcript of what was said, I will only describe their views to the extent that I feel certain of my memory. Specter's are in print in the *U.S. News and World Report* interview. Griffin and Liebeler dismissed the FBI reports as inaccurate (though I have heard on good authority that J. Edgar Hoover does not accept this view). Specter holds that these reports "reflected the doctors' comments overheard by FBI agents who were present at the autopsy. Those comments were based on factors which were originally thought to be true on the night of the autopsy, when there was relatively limited information available to the doctors actually performing the autopsy" (p.48). Nevertheless, this still seems to leave the problem: if the

Sibert-O'Neill report was an accurate account of what was found that night, is it accurate as to the location of the wound? Specter keeps saying the hole was "at the base of the back of the neck." The Sibert-O'Neill report does not say this, nor does Exhibit 397 indicate this. Later on, Specter says that he has seen "one picture of the back of a body which was represented to be the back of the President, although it was not technically authenticated. It showed a hole in the position identified in the autopsy report" (p. 53). (As far as I know, this is the first claim that someone has seen photographic evidence on the subject. I have been told that William Manchester, in his forthcoming book, will say that the autopsy photographs confirm or are consistent with the autopsy claims.)

This still does not clarify the mystery of why the FBI reports are in disagreement with the autopsy report, and why this was not taken up in the Warren Commission investigation. Sibert and O'Neill were not called to testify, though they were eyewitnesses to the autopsy. The Commission staff people have said they were aware of the discrepancy as soon as they came to work and saw the FBI reports and the autopsy report. Then why didn't they clarify this on the record by getting the autopsy surgeons to comment on the FBI's claims, and Sibert and O'Neill to comment on the doctors'? Why wasn't Dr. Humes asked what was in the preliminary draft notes he burned? (Was it, after all, an autopsy report much like what is in the Sibert-O'Neill report?) If Dr. Humes had good medical reasons for changing his mind, after his discussion on the telephone with Dr. Perry in Dallas, and after reconsidering the findings, why wasn't he asked to explain this? One gets the impression that a serious effort was being made to keep the FBI claims out of the record.

The new data and explanations may accurately reflect what happened, but still do not account for the discrepancy, or for the reason why it was kept from public view until Epstein revealed it. But even at this late date, it certainly is helpful to have the views of some of the Commission staff on this basic problem. How much more helpful it would be to have the views of Doctors Boswell, Finck and Humes and of FBI agents Sibert and O'Neill, and to have the autopsy photographs and X-rays available. (Specter is asked in the *U.S. News* interview if the photographs would not clear up the question "beyond all doubt" as to whether the hole in the back was higher or lower than the hole in the front. He answers, "They would corroborate that which is already known, which, in my opinion, has cleared up that question once and for all .... The photographs would, however, corroborate that which the autopsy surgeons testified to" [p. 53]. Since no one, except Specter, as far as we know, has seen any photographs, it is hard to see on what he bases this, except his faith in the integrity of the doctors.)

On this front, then, some further investigation has brought answers from some Commission personnel on some of the questions. I for one don't find the answers adequate, and I believe that only by having the data (the photographs and X-rays) available, and by the questioning of witnesses (the doctors and the FBI agents), will we ever have a satisfactory resolution of this fundamental basis for doubting. (At the New York debate in September 1966, Mr. Griffin posed the problem of whether we critics, who doubted the autopsy surgeons, would be any more satisfied by any additional expert testimony. For myself, I would be, if three or more eminent pathologists at leading medical schools examined the photographs and X-rays and gave their opinions.)

On the matter of the one-bullet hypothesis and bullet 399 some further investigation has also ensued. During the New York debate, Liebeler offered tentatively a different hypothesis, namely that Kennedy was shot much earlier, around Zapruder frame 180-190, and that Connally was hit by a separate bullet. This removes the inconsistency in time, and is consistent with Governor Connally's testimony. Yet this hypothesis seems to pose several problems: for example, it would then have required four bullets, two to hit Kennedy, one for Connally, and the shot that missed. Since three shells were found by the sixth floor window, where did the fourth shell go? Also, if 399 remains the bullet that struck Connally (on this theory), what became of the first bullet that struck Kennedy?

Specter insists the one-bullet hypothesis is not "a prerequisite to the Commission's conclusions that Oswald was the sole assassin." (p.56) (In this he seems to be in disagreement with some of his colleagues from the Commission.) He then claims that one can't tell when Connally was struck, so the time factor problem can't be a crucial issue. However there appears no evidence as to when Connally could not have been struck, and this does raise the problem again. A more intriguing theory is being developed by Mr. Curtis Crawford, a one-and-a-half-bullet hypothesis. To account for the condition of 399 and for Connally's wounds, Crawford suggests that Connally was wounded by both 399 and a fragment of the bullet that struck Kennedy's head and shattered. I think this would still not explain 399's pristine condition, nor does it seem entirely consistent with either the medical testimony or with the testimony of Governor and Mrs. Connally.

The recent *Ramparts* article cites some new data, which if accurate, may be very important. The authors report that they talked to a Mr. William Stinson who is an aide to Governor Connally. Stinson was present in the operating room on November 22, 1963, when the Governor was operated upon. Stinson was not interviewed by the Warren Commission. He told *Ramparts*, "The last thing they did was to remove the bullet from the governor's thigh" (pp.48-49).

If this is true, then bullet 399 did not come out of the governor, and the problem arises again, where did it come from? *Ramparts* checked with Dr. Charles Baxter, who assisted in the operation on Connally's thigh, and asked him about this. (Dr. Baxter was not questioned on this matter when the Commission interviewed him.) "He told us that bullet fragments, not an entire bullet, had been removed from the thigh" (p.49). If this is the case, it makes it more certain that 399 can't be the bullet that did the damage to Connally, since the fragments in Connally's wrist were sufficient to make the experts doubt that 399 could have been the bullet that wounded him.

Additional fragments in the thigh would really be too much, even for miraculous 399. This would force a reconsideration of the provenance of 399. It would seem that the possibilities would come down to either considering 399 as the bullet that wounded Kennedy in the back, but which did not penetrate his body (the original theory reported in the Sibert-O'Neill document), or the theory I offered, that 399 was a plant, and that it functioned as part of a conspiracy.

There has been little development on the speculation about the nature of a possible conspiracy. We critics have been attacked by various commentators because we do not agree on this score. However, I think that there is nothing surprising in disagreement given the present state of knowledge on the subject. We agree that there are fundamental weaknesses and inconsistencies in the Warren Commission case, and that something else must have happened. Our speculations as to what this something else might have been are severely restricted because of the limited data on this score collected by the Warren Commission, and the difficulty in obtaining additional data by private means.

However, I think all of us are struck by the double-Oswald material, and see in it a basis for theorizing. I have offered one possibility for interpreting this data, which I believe allows for explanation of more of the facts than other current theories. Obviously my hypothesis requires far more exploratory effort and examination before it can be considered a thorough explanation of what happened. And, of course, better explanations may come to light.

At this stage it is only to be expected that each of us working .independently will come up with different suggestions, all of which deserve consideration, and all of which may throw new light on the subject. If all critics agreed, the exploration of possibilities other than the Warren Commission's might be seriously inhibited.

I must conclude by referring to the severe criticism I have received for mentioning as rumor a theory that Kennedy's successor may have been involved. I mentioned this as one of the many theories that is heard. Unfortunately a measurable number of Americans (2 per cent according to the Harris poll) and a larger number of Europeans hold this theory. I think nothing is gained by pretending that it doesn't exist.

It is probably part of the present disenchantment with the Warren Commission, and part of the fevered speculation that will go on until a publicly satisfactory explanation of the events in Dallas is offered. Surely one of the significant arguments for a new investigation is that it might accomplish what the first one did not; that is, it could quiet the fears and rumors, and end the speculations.

Paris, October 31, 1966.

Afterword

Second Thoughts on *The Second Oswald*

The following is an excerpt from a much longer article by Richard H. Popkin that first appeared in the *St. Louis Jewish Light*, November 30, 1983.

In sum, where are we now? By this stage in history and in the accumulation of evidence I think at least the following theories are supportable by evidence, and are not disprovable:

1. The events in Dealey Plaza, Nov. 22, 1963, were designed to assassinate Gov. Connally, and Kennedy was an innocent bystander.

2. That Kennedy's assassination was designed by anti-Castro Cubans, with assistance from U.S. intelligence personnel, to precipitate another invasion of Cuba. Oswald's role was to create the *causus belli* by disappearing into the arms of Fidel Castro.

3. That Kennedy's assassination was designed and carried through by Mafia elements, because of the actions of JFK and his brother in interfering with their operations. Oswald was a bit player in this scenario, who became the main suspect.

4. That Kennedy's assassination was the result of Oswald's involvements in Russia. Oswald's activities before, during and

after his trip to Russia strongly indicate he was somebody's agent, maybe a double agent. His access to a high KGB figure in Mexico City, and the lack of interest in his activities in Mexico and Dallas on the part of the CIA and FBI again suggest his being somebody's agent. The clues of his Nov. 9, 1963 letter, his aggressive and pro-Russian remarks in Dallas just before the assassination, and his calm after his arrest are all suggestive of some kind of spy plot.

5. The Kennedy assassination was planned and carried out by Russian agents, and Nosenko was used to disinform the U.S. authorities. (Yuri Nosenko, a KGB agent then in Switzerland, contacted the CIA in early February 1964, saying he wanted to defect, and that he had all of the Russian information on Oswald.)

6. The Kennedy assassination was planned and carried out so that the Russians would be blamed and World War III would commence. Castro's speech and Nosenko's defection were attempts to defuse this.

7. The Kennedy assassination was Castro's revenge for the many ongoing attempts to assassinate him. Although Castro had publicly stated he would avenge these plots, there is nothing besides Oswald's "fake" pro-Castro activities to indicate Castro was at all carrying on any offensive efforts against his American antagonists.

8. That Kennedy was assassinated by some faction in the CIA-KGB puzzle factory as part of a power struggle between the secret leaders of these two groups. Kennedy had tried to purge the CIA after the Bay of Pigs. Allan Dulles, its fired leader, had written (or had had ghost-written) by Watergate burglar, E. Howard Hunt, *The Craft of Intelligence*, in which in early 1963, he strongly indicated our ability to stop the Communists depended on getting rid of Kennedy. Marchetti's KGB branch of the CIA may have capitalized on the opposition of Dulles, Hunt, Angleton and others to Kennedy, and ...

All of these I say are possible scenarios, supported by some evidence and not presently refutable. There are no doubt other scenarios that meet these conditions. Unless more evidence, a confession or two, some secret papers released, somebody's secret memoirs turn up we may be left at this point.

Appendices

Appendix I

The report on the autopsy by FBI agents O'Neill and Sibert.

Other FBI documents relating to the autopsy are attached. None of these documents was published by the Warren Commission.

CD-7
DL 100-10481/cv
A. AUTOPSY OF BODY OF PRESIDENT
JOHN FITZGERALD KENNEDY
FD-302 (Rev. 1-25-60)
FEDERAL BUREAU OF INVESTIGATION
Date 11/26/63

At approximately 3 p.m. on November 22, 1963, following the President's announced assassination, it was ascertained that Air Force One, the President's jet, was returning from Love Field, Dallas, Texas, flying the body back to Andrews Air Force Base, Camp Springs, Maryland. SAs FRANCIS X. O'NEILL, Jr. and JAMES W. SIBERT proceeded to Andrews Air Force Base to handle any matters which would fall within the jurisdiction of the Federal Bureau of Investigation, inasmuch as it was anticipated that a large group of both military and civilian personnel assigned to the Base would congregate at Base Operations to witness the landing of this flight.

Lt. Col. ROBERT T. BEST, Director of Law Enforcement and Security, advised the President's plane would arrive at 5:25 p.m. Subsequently, Col. BEST advised that the plane would arrive at 6:05 p.m.

At approximately 5:55 p.m. agents were advised through the Hyattsville Resident Agency that the Bureau had instructed that the agents accompany the body to the National Naval Medical Center,

On 11/22/63 at Bethesda, Maryland File # 89-30
by SAs FRANCIS X. O'NEILL, JR.;
        JAMES W. SIBERT :df 1
Date dictated 11/26/63

This document contains neither recommendations nor conclusions of the FBI. It is the property of the FBI and is loaned to your agency; it and its contents are not to be distributed outside your agency.

Bethesda, Maryland, to stay with the body and to obtain bullets reportedly in the President's body.

Immediately agents contacted Mr. JAMES ROWLEY, the Director of the U. S. Secret Service, identified themselves and made Mr. ROWLEY aware of our aforementioned instruction. Immediately following the plane's landing, Mr. ROWLEY arranged seating for Bureau agents in the third car of the White House motorcade which followed the ambulance containing the President's body to the Naval Medical Center, Bethesda, Maryland.

On arrival at the Medical Center, the ambulance stopped in front of the main entrance, at which time Mrs. JACQUELINE KENNEDY and Attorney General ROBERT KENNEDY embarked from the ambulance and entered the building. The ambulance was thereafter driven around to the rear entrance where the President's body was removed and taken into an autopsy room. Bureau agents assisted in the moving of the casket to the autopsy room. A tight security was immediately placed around the autopsy room by the Naval facility and the U. S. Secret Service. Bureau agents made contact with Mr. ROY KELLERMAN, the Assistant Secret Service Agent in Charge of the White House Detail, and advised him of the Bureau's interest in this matter.

He advised that he had already received instructions from Director ROWLEY as to the presence of Bureau agents. It will be noted that aforementioned Bureau agents, Mr. ROY KELLERMAN, Mr. WILLIAM GREER and Mr. WILLIAM O'LEARY, Secret Service agents, were the only personnel other than medical personnel present during the autopsy.

The following individuals attended the autopsy:

Adm. C. B. HOLLOWAY, U.S. Navy, Commanding Officer of the U. S. Naval Medical Center, Bethesda;

Adm. BERKLEY, U. S. Navy, the President's personal physician;

Commander JAMES J. HUMES, Chief Pathologist, Bethesda Naval Hospital, who conducted autopsy;

Capt. JAMES H. STONER, JR., Commanding Officer, U. S. Naval Medical School, Bethesda;

Mr. JOHN T. STRINGER, JR., Medical photographer;

JAMES H. EBERSOLE;

LLOYD E. RAIHE;

J. T. BOZWELL;

J. G. RUDNICKI;

PAUL K. O'CONNOR;

J. C. JENKINS;

JERROL F. CRESTER;

EDWARD F. REED;

JAMES METZLER.

During the course of the autopsy Lt. Col. P. FINCK, U. S. Army Armed Forces Institute of Pathology, arrived to assist Commander HUMES in the autopsy. In addition, Lt. Cmdr. GREGG CROSS and Captain DAVID OSBORNE, Chief of Surgery, entered the autopsy room.

Major General WEHLE, Commanding Officer of U. S. Military District, Washington, D.C., then entered the autopsy room to ascertain from the Secret Service arrangements concerning the transportation of the President's body back to the White House. AMC CHESTER H. BOYERS, U. S. Navy, visited the autopsy room during the final stages of such to type receipts given by FBI and Secret Service for items obtained.

At the termination of the autopsy, the following personnel from Gawler's Funeral Home entered the autopsy room to prepare the President's body for burial:

JOHN VAN HAESEN

EDWIN STROBLE

THOMAS ROBINSON

Mr. HAGEN

Brigadier General GODFREY McHUGH, Air Force Military Aide to the President, was also present, as was Dr. GEORGE BAKEMAN, U. S. Navy.

Arrangements were made for the performance of the autopsy by the U. S. Navy and Secret Service.

The President's body was removed from the casket in which it had been transported and was placed on the autopsy table, at which time the complete body was wrapped in a sheet and the head area contained an additional wrapping which was saturated with blood. Following the removal of the wrapping, it was ascertained that the President's clothing had been removed and it was also apparent that a tracheotomy had been performed, as well as surgery of the head area, namely, in the top of the skull. All personnel with the exception of medical officers needed in the taking of photographs and X-Rays were requested to leave the autopsy room and remain in an adjacent room.

Upon completion of X-Rays and photographs, the first incision was made at 8:15 p.m. X-Rays of the brain area which were developed and returned to the autopsy room disclosed a path of a missile which appeared to enter the back of the skull and the path of the disintegrated fragments could be observed along the right side of the skull. The largest secion [sic] of this missile as portrayed by X-Ray appeared to be behind the right frontal sinus. The next largest fragment appeared to be at the rear of the skull at the juncture of the skull bone.

The Chief Pathologist advised approximately 40 particles of disintegrated bullet and smudges indicated that the projectile had fragmentized while passing through the skull region.

During the autopsy inspection of the area of the brain, two fragments of metal were removed by Dr. HUMES, namely, one fragment
measuring 7 x 2 millimeters, which was removed from the right side of
the brain. An additional fragment of metal measuring 1 x 3 millimeters was also removed from this area, both of which were placed in a
glass jar containing a black metal top which were thereafter marked
for identification and following the signing of a proper receipt were
transported by Bureau agents to the FBI Laboratory.

During the latter stages of this autopsy, Dr. HUMES located an
opening which appeared to be a bullet hole which was below the
shoulders and two inches to the right of the middle line of the spinal
column.

This opening was probed by Dr. HUMES with the finger, at which
time it was determined that the trajectory of the missile entering at
this point had entered at a downward position of 45 to 60 degrees. Further probing determined that the distance traveled by this missile was
a short distance inasmuch as the end of the opening could be felt with
the finger.

Inasmuch as no complete bullet of any size could be located in the
brain area and likewise no bullet could be located in the back or any
other area of the body as determined by total body X-Rays and inspection revealing there was no point of exit, the individuals performing
the autopsy were at a loss to explain why they could find no bullets.

A call was made by Bureau agents to the Firearms Section of the
FBI Laboratory, at which time SA CHARLES L. KILLION advised
that the Laboratory had received through Secret Service Agent
RICHARD JOHNSON a bullet which had reportedly been found on a
stretcher in the emergency room of Parkland Hospital, Dallas, Texas.
This stretcher had also contained a stethoscope and pair of rubber
gloves. Agent JOHNSON had advised the Laboratory that it had not
been ascertained whether or not this was the stretcher which had been
used to transport the body of President KENNEDY. Agent KILLION
further described this bullet as pertaining to a 6.5 millimeter rifle
which would be approximately a 25 caliber rifle and that this bullet
consisted of a copper alloy full jacket.

Immediately following receipt of this information, this was made available to Dr. HUMES who advised that in his opinion this accounted for no bullet being located which had entered the back region, and that since external cardiac massage had been performed at Parkland Hospital, it was entirely possible that through such movement the bullet had worked its way back out of the point of entry and had fallen on the stretcher.

Also during the latter stages of the autopsy, a piece of the skull measuring 10 x 6.5 centimeters was brought to Dr. HUMES who was instructed that this had been removed from the President's skull. Immediately this section of skull was X-Rayed, at which time it was determined by Dr. HUMES that one corner of this section revealed minute metal particles and inspection of this same area disclosed a chipping of the top portion of this piece, both of which indicated that this had been the point of exit of the bullet entering the skull region.

On the basis of the latter two developments, Dr, HUMES stated that the pattern was clear that the one bullet had entered the President's back and had worked its way out of the body during external cardiac massage and that a second high velocity bullet had entered the rear of the skull and had fragmentized prior to exit through the top of the skull. He further pointed out that X-Rays had disclosed numerous fractures in the cranial area which he attributed to the force generated by the impact of the bullet in its passage through the brain area. He attributed the death of the President to a gunshot wound in the head.

The following is a complete listing of photographs and X-Rays taken by the medical authorities of the President's body. They were turned over to Mr. ROY KELLERMAN of the Secret Service. X-Rays were developed by the hospital; however, the photographs were delivered to Secret Service undeveloped:

11 X-Rays

22 4 x 5 color photographs

18 4 x 5 black and white photographs

1 roll of 120 film containing five exposures

Mr. KELLERMAN stated these items could be made available to the FBI upon request. The portion of the skull measuring 10 x 6.5 centimeters was maintained in the custody of Dr. HUMES who stated that it also could be made available for further examination. The two metal fragments removed from the brain area were hand carried by SAs SIBERT and O'NEILL to the FBI Laboratory immediately following the autopsy and were turned over to SA KURT FRAZIER.

FD-302 (Rev. 1-25-60)

FEDERAL BUREAU OF INVESTIGATION

Date 11/29/63

Mr. GERALD A. BEHN, Special Agent in Charge, White House Detail, United States Secret Service, was interviewed at his office and advised that during the President's visit to the State of Texas, then Vice President JOHNSON would always arrive at the next city to be visited ahead of the President and would join the party awaiting the President's arrival. This was accomplished by the use of two Jets; Air Force I, which carried the President; and Air Force II, carrying the Vice President. Once departing from a city, Air Force I would first take off followed by Air Force II which would thereafter pass Air Force I in flight, cruising at a faster speed, thus allowing the Vice President to arrive prior to the President and be with the greeting party.

Mr. BEHN was questioned concerning the section of the President's skull, which was brought to the National Navy Medical Center at Bethesda, Maryland after the autopsy was in progress. He advised that this section, which was measured by the Doctor performing the autopsy as being 10 x 6.5 centimeters, was found in the Presidential car on the floor between the front and rear seats. He further related that two fragments of bullets had also been found in this vehicle in the front of the car and that the windshield had been cracked by the impact of one of these fragments.

BEHN was likewise questioned concerning the location of a bullet which had been found on a stretcher at Parkland Hospital in Dallas and which had been turned over by the Secret Service to an Agent of the Federal Bureau of investigation for delivery to the FBI Laboratory.

He stated

ON 11/27/63 at Washington, D.C. File # BA 89-30
by SAs JAMES W. SIBERT & FRANCIS X. O'NEILL JR.; Mk
Date Dictated 11/27/63

This document contains neither recommendations nor conclusions of the FBI. It is the property of the FBI and is loaned to your agency; it and its contents are not to be distributed outside your agency.

Upon learning of such a bullet being found at the Dallas Hospital he inquired of a group of his Agents who had returned from the Dallas trip on the night of November 22, 1963, and Secret Service Agent RICHARD JOHNSON produced this bullet which had been handed to him by someone at the hospital who had stated that it was not known whether or not the President had been placed on the stretcher where the bullet was found.

Mr. BEHN advised that the undeveloped photographs and x-rays made during the course of the autopsy conducted at the National Naval Medical Center, Bethesda, Maryland, are in the custody of Mr. BOB BOUCK, Protective Research Section, United States Secret Service and could be made available to the Federal Bureau of Investigation on request.

FD-302 (Rev. 1-25-60)
FEDERAL BUREAU OF INVESTIGATION
Date 11/26/63

At 8:50 p.m., Mr. JAMES ROWLEY, Chief, United States Secret Service, gave to SA ELMER LEE TODD an envelope containing a bullet. This envelope and its contents were taken directly to the FBI Laboratory and delivered to SA ROBERT A. FRAZIER. The envelope was opened and initials of both SA TODD and FRAZIER were etched on the nose of the bullet for identification purposes.

On 11/22/63 at Washington, D.C. File # WFO 89-75 by SA ELMER LEE TODD :mpc Date dictated 11/26/63

This document contains neither recommendations nor conclusions of the FBI. It is the property of the FBI and is loaned to your agency; it and its contents are not to be distributed outside your agency.

Appendix II

Exhibit 385: the Commission's sketch of the path of the first bullet.

Appendix III

The testimony of Mrs. Odio.

MR. LIEBELER. My record indicates that on December 18, 1963, you were interviewed by two agents of the FBI, Mr. James P. Hosty and Bardwell D. Odum. Do you remember that?

MRS. ODIO. That's correct.

MR. LIEBELER. It is my understanding that they interviewed you at your place of work, is that correct?

MRS. ODIO. Yes.

MR. LIEBELER. Do you remember approximately what they asked you and what you told them?

MRS. ODIO. Not exactly, but I think I can recall the conversation.

MR. LIEBELER. Would you give us the content of that conversation, as best you can recall it?

MRS. ODIO. They told me they were coming because of the assassination of President Kennedy, that they had news that I knew or I had known Lee Harvey Oswald. And I told them that I had not known him as Lee Harvey Oswald, but that he was introduced to me as Leon Oswald. And they showed me a picture of Oswald and a picture of Ruby. I did not know Ruby, but I did recall Oswald. They asked me about my activities in JURE. That is the Junta Revolutionary, and it is led by Manolo Ray. I told him that I did belong to this organization because my father and mother had belonged in Cuba, and I had seen him (Ray) in Puerto Rico recently, and that I knew him personally, and that I did belong to JURE. They asked me about the members here in Dallas, and I told him a few names of the Cubans here. They asked me to tell the story about what happened in my house.

MR. LIEBELER. Who was it that you had seen in Puerto Rico?

MRS. ODIO. Mr. Ray, I had seen. He was a very close friend of my father and mother. He hid in my house several times in Cuba.

So they asked me to tell him how I came to know Oswald, and I told them that it was something very brief and I could not recall the time, exact date. I still can't. We more or less have established that it was the end of September. And, of course, my sister had recognized him at the same time I did, but I did not say anything to her. She came very excited one day and said, "That is the man that was in my house." And I said, "Yes; I remember."

MR. LIEBELER. Tell us all the circumstances surrounding the event when Oswald came to your house.

MRS. ODIO. Well, I had been having little groups of Cubans coming to my house who have been asking me to help them in JURE. They were going to open a revolutionary paper here in Dallas. And I told them at the time I was very busy with my four children, and I would help, in other things like selling bonds to help buy arms for Cuba. And I said I would help as much as I could. Those are my activities before Oswald came. Of course, all the Cubans knew that I was involved in JURE, but it did not have a lot of sympathy in Dallas and I was criticized because of that.

MR. LIEBELER. Because of what now?

MRS. ODIO. Because I was sympathetic with Ray and this movement. Ray has always had the propaganda that he is a leftist and that he is Castro without Castro. So at that time I was planning to move over to Oak Cliff because it was much nearer to my work in Irving. So we were all involved in this moving business, and my sister Annie, who at the time was staying with some American friends, had come over that weekend to babysit for me. It either was a Thursday or a Friday. It must have been either one of those days, in the last days of

September. And I was getting dressed to go out to a friend's house, and she was staying to babysit.

Like I said, the doorbell rang and so she went over—she had a housecoat on—she wasn't dressed properly—and came back and said, "Sylvia, there are three men at the door, and one seems to be an American, the other two seem to be Cubans. Do you know them?" So I put a housecoat on and stood at the door. I never opened my door unless I know who they are, because I have had occasions where Cubans have introduced themselves as having arrived from Cuba and known my family, and I never know. So I went to the door, and he said, "Are you Sarita Odio?" And I said, "I am not. That is my sister studying at the University of Dallas. I am Sylvia." Then he said, "Is she the oldest?" And I said, "No; I am the oldest." And he said, "It is you we are looking for." So he said, "We are members of JURE." This at the time struck me funny, because their faces did not seem familiar, and I asked them for their names. One of them said his name was Leopoldo. He said that was his war name. In all this underground, everybody has a war name. This was done for safety in Cuba. So when everybody came to exile, everyone was known by their war names.

And the other one did give me his name, but I can't recall. I have been trying to recall. It was something like Angelo. I have never been able to remember, and I couldn't be exact on this name, but the other one I am exact on; I remember perfectly.

MR. LIEBELER. Let me ask you this before you go ahead with the story. Which one of the men told you that they were members of JURE and did most of the talking? Was it the American?

MRS. ODIO. The American had not said a word yet.

MR. LIEBELER. Which one of the Cubans?

MRS. ODIO. The American was in the middle. They were leaning against the staircase. There was a tall one. Let me tell you, they both looked very greasy like the kind of low Cubans, not educated at all. And one was on the heavier side and had black hair. I recall one of them had glasses, if I remember. We have been trying to establish, my sister and I, the identity of this man. And one of them, the tall was the one called Leopoldo.

MR. LIEBELER. He did most of the talking?

MRS. ODIO. He did most of the talking. The other one kept quiet, and the American, we will call him Leon, said just a few little words in Spanish, trying to be cute, but very few like "Hola," like that in Spanish.

MR. LIEBELER. Did you have a chain on the door, or was the door completely opened?

MRS. ODIO. I had a chain.

MR. LIEBELER. Was the chain fastened?

MRS. ODIO. No; I unfastened it after a little while when they told me they were members of JURE, and were trying to let me have them come into the house. When I said no, one of them said, "We are very good friends of your father." This struck me, because I didn't think my father could have such kind of friends, unless he knew them from anti-Castro activities. He gave me so many details about where they saw my father and what activities he was in. I mean, they gave me almost incredible details about things that somebody who knows him really would or that somebody informed well knows. And after a little while, after they mentioned my father, they started talking about the American. He said, "You are working in the underground." And I said, "No, I am sorry to say I am not working in the underground." And he said, "We wanted you to meet this American. His name is Leon Oswald."

He repeated it twice. Then my sister Annie by that time was standing near the door. She had come to see what was going on. And they introduced him as an American who was very much interested in the Cuban cause. And let me see, if I recall exactly what they said about him. I don't recall at the time I was at the door things about him.

I recall a telephone call that I had the next day from the so-called Leopoldo, so I cannot remember the conversation at the door about this American.

MR. LIEBELER. Did your sister hear this man introduced as Leon Oswald?

MRS. ODIO. She says she doesn't recall. She could not say that it is true. I mean, even though she said she thought I had mentioned the name very clearly, and I had mentioned the names of the three men.

MR. LIEBELER. But she didn't remember it?

MRS. ODIO. No; she said I mentioned it, because I made a comment. This I don't recall. I said, "I am going to see Antonio Alentado," which is one of the leaders of the JURE here in Dallas. And I think I just casually said, "I am going to mention these names to him to see if he knows any of them." But I forgot about them.

MR. LIEBELER. Did your sister see the men?

MRS. ODIO. She saw the three of them.

MR. LIEBELER. Have you discussed this with her since that time?

MRS. ODIO. I just had to discuss it because it was bothering me. I just had to know.

MR. LIEBELER. Did she think it was Oswald?

MRS. ODIO. Well, her reaction to it when Oswald came on television, she almost passed out on me, just like I did the day at work when I learned about the assassination of the President. Her reaction was so obvious that it was him, I mean. And my reaction, we remember Oswald the day he came to my house because he had not shaved and he had a kind of a very, I don't know how to express it, but some little hairs like if you haven't shaved, but it is not a thick moustache, but some kind of shadow.

That is something I noticed. And he was wearing—the other ones were wearing white dirty shirts, but he was wearing a long sleeved shirt.

MR. LIEBELER. What kind of shirt was it, a white shirt?

MRS. ODIO. No; it was either green or blue, and he had it rolled up to here.

MR. LIEBELER. Almost to his elbows?

MRS. ODIO. No; less than that, just the ends of the sleeves.

MR. LIEBELER. Did he have a tie?

MRS. ODIO. No tie.

MR. LIEBELER. Was it a sport shirt, or working shirt?

MRS. ODIO. He had it open. I don't know if he had a collar or not, but it was open. And the other one had a white undershirt. One of them was very hairy. Where was I? I want to remember everything.

MR. LIEBELER. You mentioned when your sister saw Oswald's picture on television that she almost passed out. Did she recognize him, do you know, as the man that had been in the apartment?

MRS. ODIO. She said, "Sylvia, you know that man?" And I said, "Yes," and she said, "I know him." "He was the one that came to our door, and it couldn't be so, could it?"

That was our first interview. We were very much concerned after that. We were concerned and very scared, because I mean, it was such a shock.

This man, the other one, the second Cuban, took out a letter written in Spanish, and the content was something like we represent the revolutionary council, and we are making a big movement to buy arms for Cuba and to help overthrow the dictator Castro, and we want you to translate this letter and write it in English and send a lot of them to different industries to see if we get some results.

This same petition had been asked of me by Alentado who was one of the leaders of JURE, here in Dallas. He had made this petition to me, "Sylvia, let's write letters to different industries to see if we can raise some money." I had told him too, I was very busy. So I asked and I said, "Are you sent by Alentado? Is this a petition?"

MR. LIEBELER. You mentioned this Alentado who was one of the JURE representatives here in Dallas. Is that his full name?

MRS. ODIO. His name is Antonio.

MR. LIEBELER. Do you know a man by the name of George Rodriguez Alvareda?

MRS. ODIO. Yes.

MR. LIEBELER. Who is he?

MRS. ODIO. He is another member of JURE. And at the time, a little after that, after December, I was more in contact with him, and I will tell you why later. They are all members of JURE here in Dallas, working hard.

And so I asked him if they were sent by him, and he said, "No." And I said, "Do you know Eugenio?" This is the war name for—. That is his war name and everybody underground knows him as Eugenio. So I didn't mention his real name. He didn't know.

MR. LIEBELER. Who did you ask this?

MRS. ODIO. I asked these men when they came to the door—I asked if they had been sent by Alentado, because I explained to them that he had already asked me to do the letters and he said no. And I said, "Were you sent by Eugenio," and he said no. And I said, "Where [sic] you sent by Ray," and he said no. And I said, "Well, is this on your own?" And he said, "'We have just come from New Orleans and we have been trying to get this organized, this movement organized down there, and this is on our own, but we think we could do some kind of work." This was all talked very fast, not as slow as I am saying it now. And he put the letter back in his pocket when I said no. And then I think I asked something to the American, trying to be nice, "Have you ever been to Cuba?" And he said, "No, I have never been to Cuba."

And I said, "Are you interested in our movement?" He said, "Yes."

This I had not remembered until lately. I had not spoken much to him and I said, "If you will excuse me, I have to leave," and I repeated, "I am going to write to my father and tell him you have come to visit me." And he said, "Is he still in the Isle of Pines?" And I think that was the extent of the conversation. They left, and I saw them through the window leaving in a car. I can't recall the car. I have been trying to.

MR. LIEBELER. Do you know which one of the men was driving?

MRS. ODIO. The tall one, Leopoldo.

MR. LIEBELER. Leopoldo?

MRS. ODIO. Yes; oh, excuse me, I forgot something very important. They kept mentioning that they had come to visit me at such a time of night; it was almost 9 o'clock because they were leaving for a trip. And two or three times they said the same thing.

They said, "We may stay until tomorrow, or we might leave tomorrow night, but please excuse us for the hour." And he mentioned two or three times they were leaving for a trip. I didn't ask where, and I had the feeling they were leaving for Puerto Rico or Miami.

MR. LIEBELER. But they did not indicate where they were going?

MRS. ODIO. The next day Leopoldo called me. I had gotten home from work, so I imagine it must have been Friday. And they had come on Thursday. I have been trying to establish that. He was trying to get fresh with me that night. He was trying to be too nice, telling me that I was pretty, and he started like that. That is the way he started the conversation. Then he said, "What do you think of the American?" And I said, "I didn't think anything."

And he said, "You know our idea is to introduce him to the underground in Cuba, because he is great, he is kind of nuts." This was more or less—I can't repeat the exact words, because he was kind of nuts. He told us we don't have any guts, you Cubans, because President Kennedy should have been assassinated after the Bay of Pigs, and some Cubans should have done that, because he was the one that was holding the freedom of Cuba actually. And I started getting a little upset with the conversation.

And he said, "It is so easy to do it." He has told us. And he (Leopoldo) used two or three bad words, and I wouldn't repeat it in Spanish. And he repeated again they were leaving for a trip and they would like very much to see me on their return to Dallas. Then he mentioned something more about Oswald. They called him Leon. He never mentioned the name Oswald.

MR. LIEBELER. He never mentioned the name of Oswald on the telephone?

MRS. ODIO. He never mentioned his last name. He always referred to the American or Leon.

MR. LIEBELER. Did he mention his last name the night before?

MRS. ODIO. Before they left I asked their names again, and he mentioned their names again.

MR. LIEBELER. But he did not mention Oswald's name except as Leon?

MRS. ODIO. On the telephone conversation he referred to him as Leon or an American. He said he had been a Marine and he was so interested in helping the Cubans, and he was terrific. That is the words he more or less used, in Spanish, that he was terrific. And I don't remember what else he said, or something that he was coming back or something and he would see me. It's been a long time and I don't remember too well, that is more or less what he said.

(X1:369-73)

Appendix IV

The FBI's report reviewing Mrs. Odio's story, dated September 9, 1964.

FD-302 (Rev. 1-25-60)
FEDERAL BUREAU OF INVESTIGATION
Date September 10, 1964

SYLVIA ODIO advised that she resides with her four small children in a one family house at 4223 West Levers Lane, Dallas, Texas. She stated that she is currently employed by Knob Associates, Incorporated, 250 Decorative Center, Dallas, Texas.

Miss SYLIVA EUGENIA ODIO was born on May 4, 1937, at Havana, Cuba. She speaks English fluently.

SYLVIA ODIO noted that she is planning to move with her four children around the end of September to Miami, Florida, where she intends to unite her nine brothers and sisters into one family. She stated she does not have a house located as yet in Miami, but her oldest brother, CESAR ODIO, presently resides at 1600 Southwest 82nd Place, Miami, Florida.

Miss ODIO stated she is from a large family consisting of ten brothers and sisters, namely, CESAR, AMADOR, JAVIER, FREDDY, JORGE, SARA, ANNIE, MARY LOU, CRISTINA and herself. Her parents, AMADOR ODIO-PADRON and SARA DEL TORO, are still in

Cuba. Her father is in jail on the Isle of Pines, Cuba, for being an enemy of the Castro Government. Her mother is now in Santiago de Cuba, Oriente, Cuba. She stated that all of her brothers and sisters are in the United States. Several of the younger brothers and sisters are now in an orphanage in Dallas. All of the brothers and sisters will be reunited in Miami, with the exception of one sister, SARA, who recently married JACOB MEIER and who will continue to reside in Dallas.

On 9/9/64 at Dallas, Texas File # DL 100-10461 by Special Agent RICHARD J. BURNETT/ jtf

Date dictated 9/9/64

This document contains neither recommendations nor conclusions of the FBI. It is the property of the FBI and is loaned to your agency; it and its contents are not to be distributed outside your agency.

Miss ODIO stated her father, AMADOR ODIO-PADRON, was active in the Cuban underground assisting CASTRO in the revolution against BATISTA. Her father was exiled twice previously from Cuba during BATISTA's era. After FIDEL CASTRO came to power in Cuba, her father, realizing too late that CASTRO was a Communist, joined the Cuban underground and fought against the CASTRO regime. He and his family used to hide members of the Cuban underground who were fighting CASTRO.

ODIO stated that she married GUILLERMO HERRERA, a Cuban in Havana, Cuba, in 1957. In 1960, her husband, their children and she were able to leave Cuba and went to Ponce, Puerto Rico, via Miami, Florida, where they spent a few days being processed by U. S. Immigration authorities.

She and her family then resided at Ponce, Puerto Rico, until she left for Dallas, Texas, in March 1963, to join her sister, SARA, who was at that time a student in the University of Dallas. She left her children in Puerto Rice until she could make living arrangements for them with her in Dallas. Miss ODIO stated she had obtained a divorce from her husband in both Ponce and San Juan, Puerto Rico, in early 1963. She stated due to her marital problems, her parents being in jail in Cuba, and her brothers and sisters all scattered throughout the United States, she had developed a nervous condition but same had not affected her mentality, and she does not suffer from illusions.

Miss ODIO stated in regard to previous information furnished her to the President's Commission regarding the visit to her apartment, around the latter part of September, 1963, of three individuals, one of whom she believes was LEE HARVEY OSWALD, she has the following information to furnish:

She advised that she has tried and tried to definitely determine the exact date these three persons came to her apartment. She stated that she has discussed this matter with her sister, ANNIE, who was in her apartment when these three men came to her residence.

She stated her sister, ANNIE, normally came to her apartment on Friday to baby-sit for her, as she, SYLVIA. normally went out that night of the week; however, ANNIE had come early this particular week, and both she and her sister now believe that she, ANNIE, had arrived on Thursday, September 26, 1963.

Miss ODIO remembers that she moved from her apartment at 1084 Magellan Circle, Casa View, Dallas, Texas, on Monday, September 30, 1963, to avoid having to pay any additional rent for October at this address. She stated she does not go out on Sundays and would have been home on Sunday. September 29, 1963. On Saturdays, Miss ODIO stated that she is normally so tired that she stays home all day and would have been home on Saturday, September 28, 1963.

Miss ODIO stated that she received the one telephone call from the previous night's visitor, who had identified himself to her as "LEOPOLDO", after she returned home from work. Accordingly, this telephone call would have had to be on either Thursday, September 26, 1963, or Friday, September 27, 1963; however, she stated that Friday, September 27, 1963, would be her best recollection of the exact day.

She stated that the three men, one of whom is believed by her to have been OSWALD, were most probably at her apartment on Thurs-

day night, September 26, 1963. She stated that if it was not Thursday
night, September 26, 1963, then it would have been Wednesday, September 25, 1963, but she considers the Thursday date to be the most
probable date.

Miss ODIO advised that the Cuban anti-CASTRO group known as
the Directorate Revolucionario Estudiantil, more commonly referred
to as the "DRE", has never to her knowledge been au organized group
in the Dallas area.

She stated that while a resident of Ponce, Puerto Rico, she had attended the organizing meeting of "JURE" held in early 1963 at Juana
Diaz, Puerto Rico, a town located near Ponce, Puerto Rico. She stated
that she was one of the original members of this organization.

Miss ODIO stated that if the two other individuals who visited her
home on the night in question were truly members of the "JURE",
then MANOLO RAY, head of this group, should positively know the
identity of any such "JURE" member who uses the war name of
"LEOPOLDO".

Miss ODIO stated that in her own mind she rather doubts that
these two other visitors were actually members of "JURE". She stated
that she bases this doubt on the fact that these two unknown men appeared to her to be Mexicans rather than Cubans. She stated that
their skin was "olive" colored, which skin tone is common among
Mexicans and not among Cubans.

She stated that in their approximately fifteen minute conversation
on the night in question, she cannot recall any phrases or words in
Spanish used by "LEOPOLDO" or the other man which would indicate
that they were not actually Cubans, but instead Mexicans. She noted
that she does not recall any idiomatic phrases used by them at that
time, as she did not then question their authenticity.

She stated that she would probably have never given much
thought to their visit if it had not been for the subsequent assassination of President KENNEDY. When she first heard of President
KENNEDY's assassination, at work, on the afternoon of November 22,
1963, she immediately recalled the visit of the three men to her home
in late September, 1963, and thought it very possible that they might

have been responsible, as one had mentioned that night that President
KENNEDY should have been killed by the Cubans.

She stated she became very nervous regarding this possibility and
feared that the Cuban exiles might be accused of the President's death
and, upon dwelling on this thought, had fainted at work and was taken
to the hospital in Irving, Texas.Miss ODIO emphatically denied that
she had ever told Mrs. C. L. CONNELL that LEE HARVEY OSWALD
had made talks to small groups of Cuban refugees in Dallas. She simi-
larly denied knowledge of ever telling Mrs. CONNELL that a Cuban
associate of hers had called anyone in New Orleans regarding
OSWALD, in which this Cuban friend had been advised that OSWALD
was a double agent attempting to infiltrate Cuban exile groups.

Miss ODIO stated that a gun seller called JOHNNY MARTIN had
spoken before small groups of Cuban refugees in Dallas, and she believes she had mentioned this person's name to Mrs. CONNELL; however; she does not know what Mrs. CONNELL is talking about in regard to the alleged telephone call to New Orleans where a person was
discussed who might be a double agent trying to infiltrate Cuban refugee groups.

In reply to a question as to why Mrs. CONNELL would attribute
such a statement to her, Miss ODIO stated that, "You would have to be
a woman to understand". She stated that Mrs. CONNELL and she had
been friends, but due to personal reasons, they had had a falling out.
She believes that Mrs. CONNELL in attributing the aforementioned
information to her was using a "double-edged knife", that is, she was
trying to help in the investigation of the assassination and at the same
time was trying to embarrass or get her, Miss ODIO in trouble.

In regard to the information attributed to her by Mrs. CONNELL,
Miss ODIO noted that she most certainly would have mentioned these
facts to FBI Agents when they first interviewed her if she had such
knowledge of same, as she fully realizes the importance of such information, if true.

Miss ODIO stated she had not previously contacted the FBI with
her information about the three visitors who had come to her home in
September, 1963, as she had not considered it pertinent at the time

and did not want to bother the Government investigative agencies with what they might consider a "nut" complaint when they were undoubtedly so busy with other investigative matters pertaining to the assassination. She stated that she might have eventually proceeded on her own initiative to bring this incident to the attention of the appropriate authorities, but she still considers her information meager, and even unimportant, due to the very short duration of her conversation with the three visitors to her apartment in late September, 1963.

Miss ODIO stated she still personally believes that it was LEE HARVEY OSWALD who was the third man who accompanied the two self-identified Cubans to her apartment; however, she stated that she has seen so many pictures of LEE HARVEY OSWALD since the assassination of President KENNEDY that she is getting confused on this point at this late date, and added that even though she thinks it was LEE HARVEY OSWALD, it may not have been.

(XXVI: 85-38)

Appendix V

J. Edgar Hoover's letter to the Commission concerning Mrs. Odio's visitors.

September 21, 1964
BY COURIER SERVICE

Honorable J. Lee Rankin
General Counsel
The President's Commission
200 Maryland Avenue, N. E.
Washington, D.C.

Dear Mr. Rankin:

Reference is made to your letter dated August 28, 1964, dealing with the claim of Sylvia Odio that Lee Harvey Oswald and two other individuals visited at her apartment in Dallas, Texas, on September 26 or 27, 1963. Sylvia Odio in testifying before the Commission stated that the man believed by her to be Lee Harvey Oswald was introduced to her as "Leon Oswald."

In connection with investigation requested in letter of reference, there are enclosed two copies each of memoranda dated September 8,

September 10 and September 11, 1964. There are also enclosed two copies each of a memorandum dated September 14, 1964 and the eighteen attachments thereto.

On September 16, 1964, we located one Loran Eugene Hall at Johnsondale, California. Hall has been identified as a participant in numerous anti-Castro activities. He advised that in September, 1963, he was at Dallas, Texas, soliciting aid in connection with an anti-Castro cause. He recalled meeting a Cuban woman, Mrs. Odio who lived in a garden-type apartment at 1080 Magelland Circle, Dallas, Texas. He said that at the time of his visit he was accompanied by Lawrence Howard, a Mexican-American from East Los Angeles and William Seymour from Arizona. He denied that Lee Harvey Oswald was with him during his visit to Mrs. Odio's apartment in September, 1963.

Hall stated that William Seymour is similar in appearance to Lee Harvey Oswald and that Seymour speaks only a few words of Spanish. In connection with the revelations of Hall, you will note that the name Loran Hall bears some phonetic resemblance to the name Leon Oswald.

We have obtained photographs of Loran Hall and will attempt to obtain photographs of William Seymour and Lawrence Howard for display to Mrs. Odio. We are continuing our investigation into the claims of Sylvia Odio with particular emphasis on efforts to determine if Hall, Howard and Seymour may be identical with the three individuals who visited her in late September, 1963. The results of our inquiries in this regard will be promptly furnished to you.

Sincerely yours,

Enclosures—44
(XXVI:834-35)

Appendix VI

The FBI's later report on Mrs. Odio's visitors that was not published by the Warren Commission. (From National Archives: Commission Document No. 1553.)

Miami, Florida
October 2, 1964

LEE HARVEY OSWALD

It is recalled that SYLVIA ODIO has advised that on an evening in the latter part of September, 1963, she was visited at her apartment in Dallas, Texas, by two Cubans or Mexicans, accompanied by an American whom she believed to be LEE HARVEY OSWALD.

LORAN EUGENE HALL, upon interview on September 16, 1964 at Johnsondale, California, stated he had been in Dallas, Texas, in September, 1963 in the company of LAWRENCE HOWARD and WILLIAM SEYMOUR, and has contacted many Cubans in the Dallas area, including a Cuban woman, a Mrs. ODIO, who lived in apartment A, located on Magellan Circle, Dallas in the same building with a Cuban friend of HALL, named KIKI FERROR. During a second interview on September 20, 1964, HALL stated that during his visit in Dallas in September, 1963, he was accompanied by LAWRENCE HOWARD and a Cuban whom he knew as "WAHITO," and was not accompanied at that time by WILLIAM SEYMOUR. He also said he recalled no contact with ODIO.

Upon interview at Los Angeles, California on September 20, 1964, LAWRENCE JOHN HOWARD advised that he accompanied HALL to Dallas, Texas, in September, 1963 with a Cuban refugee named CELLIOS ALBAS who was also known by the name "QUARITO." HOWARD recalled no contact with a Cuban woman named ODIO at an apartment on Magellan Circle in Dallas.

WILLIAM SEYMOUR of Phoenix, Arizona, during interview on September 18, 1964, stated he and LAWRENCE HALL were in Dallas, Texas in October, 1963, rather than September, 1963, and SYLVIA ODIO was unknown to him.

Review of record of Beach Welding and Supplies Company, Miami Beach, Florida, on September 22, 1964, confirmed WILLIAM SEYMOUR's employment with that company throughout the period September 5 to October 10, 1963.

On September 24, 1964, CELLO SERGIO CASTRO ALBA, employed at the South Florida Sugar Company, Belle Glade, Florida, stated he had traveled with LORAN HALL and LAWRENCE HOWARD from California to Dallas, Texas, to Miami, Florida in September, 1963, but he had not met any person at Dallas named ODIO, nor had he heard the name ODIO mentioned by HALL or HOWARD in Dallas.

On October 1, 1964, SYLVIA ODIO, presently residing at 1711 S.W. 83rd Avenue, Miami, Florida, stated she had moved to Miami from Dallas, Texas, with her four small children, about a week ago.

Mrs. ODIO was shown photographs of LORAN EUGENE HALL, taken at Wichita, Kansas on December 16, 1961; LAWRENCE J. HOWARD taken at Key West, Florida on December 4, 1962; WILLIAM HOUSTON SEYMOUR taken in March, 1959 at San Diego, California; and CELIO SERGIO CASTRO ALBA taken in November, 1961 at Miami. Florida.

Upon viewing the photographs of HALL, HOWARD, SEYMOUR and CASTRO, Mrs. ODIO stated that none of these individuals were identical with the three persons including the individual she believed to be OSWALD, who had come to her apartment in Dallas in the last week of September, 1968. She said she is not certain that she could identify photographs of the two individuals accompanying the one she believed to be OSWALD, because of the passage of time since the incident and because photographs sometime differ from the real appearance of an individual.

Mrs. ODIO added she did believe, however, she could recognize the individual who gave his name as LEOPOLDO. She indicated that the photograph of CELIO CASTRO was similar to the appearance of LEOPOLDO but that LEOPOLDO's hairline was receding at the temples. She also thought that the photo of CELIO CASTRO did not give the Mexican appearance that she recalled LEOPOLDO to have.

Mrs. ODIO stated she did not know anyone named KIKI FERRER, or FERROR, either resident in the apartment building at 1084 Magellan Circle, where she resided, or elsewhere. She stated there was a Cuban family of man, wife and two children with the surname MASFERRER, who also lived in the Crestwood Apartments on Magellan Circle, about 5 or 6 buildings down from the building in which Mrs. ODIO lived. She said that on occasion the Cuban families living in the Crestwood Apartments would have get-togethers and she recalled that on one occasion the son of the aforementioned MASFERRER became involved in a fight with another individual and the get-together deteriorated into a general disturbance to which the police were called. She stated she did not know the first name of Mr. MASFERRER.

Also on October 1, 1964, the photographs described hereinbefore were displayed to ANNIE LAURIE ODIO, younger sister of SYLVIA ODIO, who stated she had opened the door of the ODIO apartment in Dallas to the three individuals including the one believed to be LEE HARVEY OSWALD, who called at the apartment in the last week of September, 1964. ANNIE LAURIE ODIO stated none of the photographs appeared similar to the three individuals in her recollection. When telephonically contacted on the morning of October 1, 1964 in order to arrange an interview, SYLVIA ODIO advised that she had an appointment at 11:30 AM that date with her doctor. The interview was then set for 1:00 PM. Shortly after making this arrangement for interview, Mr. MAURICE FERRE, a member of the FERRE family with extensive industrial holdings in South Florida and Puerto Rico, contacted the Miami Office of the Federal Bureau of Investigation to state he is a personal friend of SYLVIA ODIO. He wished to advise that ODIO was then under the care of Dr. IRWIN JACOBS, psychiatrist, at Miami and had attempted suicide during the past week.

Appendix VII

Oswald's letter to the Russian Embassy.

FROM: LEE H. OSWALD, P.O. BOX 6225, DALLAS, TEXAS
            MARINA NICHILAYEVA OSWALD, SOVIET CITIZEN

TO: CONSULAR DIVISION,EMBASSY U.S.S.R
WASHINGTON, D.C.

NOV. 9, 1963

Dear Sirs:

This is to inform you of recent events since my meetings with comrade Kostin in the Embassy of the Soviet Union, Mexico City, Mexico.

I was unable to remain in Mexico indefinitely because of my Mexican visa restrictions which was for 15 days only. I could not take a chance on requesting a new visa unless I used my real name, so I returned to the United States.

I had not planned to contact the Soviet embassy in Mexico so they were unprepared, had I been able to reach the Soviet Embassy in Havana as planned, the embassy there would have had time to complete our business.

Of course the Soviet embassy was not at fault, they were, as I say unprepared, the Cuban consulate was guilty of a gross breach of regulations, I am glad he has since been replaced.

The Federal Bureau of Investigation is not now interested in my activities in the progressive organization "Fair Play For Cuba Committee", of which I was secretary in New Orleans (state Louisiana) since I no longer reside in that state. However, the F.B.I. has visited us here in Dallas, Texas, on November 1st. Agent James P. Hasty warned me that if I engaged in F.P.C.C. activities in Texas the F.B.I. will again take an "interest" in me.

This agent also "suggested" to Marina Nichilayeva that she could remain in the United States under F.B.I. "protection", that is, she could defect from the Soviet Union, of course, I and my wife strongly protested these tactics by the notorious F.B.I.

Please inform us of the arrival of our Soviet entrance visa's as soon as they come.

Also, this is to inform you of the birth, on October 20, 1963 of a DAUGHTER, AUDREY MARINA OSWALD in DALLAS, TEXAS, to my wife.

Respectfully,
(XVI:33)

Appendix VIII

The FBI report on Miss Dowling of Dobbs House.

On December 6, 1963, Mary Adda Dowling, 617 West 10th, then employed by Skillern's Drug Store No. 41, Preston Road and Forest Lane, stated she was formerly employed by Dobbs House, 1221 North Beckley, during daytime hours. She professed to recognize pictures of Oswald as a person who had eaten breakfast at the restaurant usually between 7:00 and 7:30 AM. She related she recalled the person now recognized as Oswald was last seen by her in the restaurant at about 10:00 AM, Wednesday, November 20, 1963, at which time he was "nasty" and used curse words in connection with his order.

She went on to relate Officer J. D. Tippit was in the restaurant as was his habit at about that time each morning and "shot a glance at Oswald." She said there was no indication, however, they knew each other. Miss Dowling professed not to have known Jack Ruby as a customer, but said she had heard from another employee he was a night customer.

With reference to the allegation of Miss Dowling that Oswald was in the restaurant at about 10:00 AM, November 20, 1963, it is noted Roy S. Truly, Warehouse Manager, Texas School Book Depository, advised Special Agent Nat A. Pinkston on November 29, 1963, that Oswald's working hours were from 8:00 AM to 4:45 PM, with a lunch period from 12:00 noon to 12:45 PM. He said, however, there was no punch time clock.

On November 25, 1963, A. S. Aiken, Bookkeeper, Texas School Book Depository, made available copies of payroll records which reflected Oswald worked an eight-hour day on November 20, 1963.

(XXVI:516)

Appendix IX

Deputy Sheriff Craig's report on a second Oswald.

FORM 114 SUP. INV.
COUNTY OF DALLAS
SHERIFF'S DEPARTMENT
SUPPLEMENTARY INVESTIGATION REPORT
Name of Complainant Serial No.
ASSASSINATION OF PRESIDENT KENNEDY

Offense
           Officer Roger Craig,
           Dallas County Deputy Sheriff.

DETAILS OF OFFENSE, PROGRESS OF INVESTIGATION, ETC.:
(Investigation Officer must sign)
Date Nov 23, 1963   19_____
I was standing in front of the Sheriff's Office at 505 Main Street, Dallas, Texas, watching President Kennedy pass in the motorcade. I was watching the rest of the motorcade a few seconds after President Kennedy passed where I was standing when I heard a rifle shot and a few seconds later a second and then a third shot. At the retort of the first shot, I started running around the corner and Officer Buddy

Walthers and I ran across Houston Street and ran up the terrace on Elm Street and into the railroad yards. We made a round through the railroad yards and I returned to Elm Street by the Turnpike sign at which time Officer Walthers told me that a bullet had struck the curb on the south side of Elm Street. I crossed to Elm with Deputy C. L. Lummie Lewis to search for a spot where a shell might have hit. About this time I heard a shrill whistle and I turned around and saw a white male running down the hill from the direction of the Texas School Book Depository Building and I saw what I think was a light colored Rambler Station wagon with luggage rack on top pull over to the curb and this subject who had come running down the hill get into this car. The man driving this station wagon was a dark complected white male. I tried to get across Elm Street to stop the car and talk with subjects, but the traffic was so heavy I could not make it. I reported this incident at once to a secret service officer whose name I do not know, then I left this area and went at once to the building and assisted in the search of the building. Later that afternoon, I heard that the City had a suspect in custody and I called and reported the information about the suspect running down the hill and getting into a car to Captain Fritz and was requested to come at once to City Hall. I went to the City Hall and identified the subject they had in custody as being the same person I saw running down this hill and get into the station wagon and leave the scene.

(XIX:524)

Footnotes

1. An independent prepared Index by Sylvia Meagher has been published by Scarecrow Press, 275 Park Avenue South, New York. This Index is extremely useful. It consists of a subject index, a name index, and a breakdown of the names by descriptive categories as to how these persons are connected with the case. This index should do much to advance research into the subject.

2. For example, an independent researcher, Mr. Jones Harris, has given me the following report:

"In March 1966, I interviewed in Dallas a Mr. January who had been manager of Red Bird Air Field at the time of the assassination. Mr. January told me that on Wednesday, November 20, 1963, three people turned up at the airport. Two of them, a heavy-set young man and a girl, got out of their car and spoke to him, leaving a young man sitting in the front of the car. The couple inquired as to the possibility of hiring a Cessna 310 on Friday the 22nd to take them to the Yucatan peninsula. They asked how far the Cessna could travel without refueling. How fast did the plane travel? Would they have to stop in Mexico City? January replied that it would be necessary and this seemed to suit their plans.

"They told January that they wanted to be back at Red Bird Field on Sunday. January did not believe that they could afford the flight. Privately, he suspected that they might want to hijack his plane and go on to Cuba. He decided not to rent them the plane even if they turned up with the money before the flight.

"He never saw the three people again. But on Friday when he saw Oswald on TV he was certain he had seen him before. Then he remembered the young man sitting in the front seat of the car and was convinced that it had been Oswald."

Illustrations

Photograph taken by witness Howard Brennan, showing the positions of spectators at the Depository during the assassination

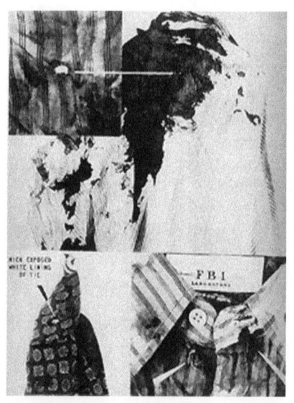

View of the back of President Kennedy's shirt with close-up of a bullet entrance hole. Lower two photographs show a projectile exit hole in the collar and nick in the right side of the tie

The tower used to simulate Oswald's alleged "sniper's nest" in the Depository

Billy Lovelady

Printed in the USA
CPSIA information can be obtained
at www.ICGtesting.com
LVHW050942220624
783734LV00008B/222